Positive Culture Wins

Gary Wilbers

Copyright © 2018 Gary Wilbers
All rights reserved.
ISBN: 0692075089
ISBN-13: 9780692075081

WHAT PEOPLE ARE SAYING

"...he combines decades of experiences garnered during his career growing businesses and teams to teach you how you can do the same in your business and with your teams."

"Gary Wilbers is a natural leader, a successful business person and a wonderful human being. In Positive Culture Wins he combines decades of experiences garnered during his career growing businesses and teams to teach you how you can do the same in your business and with your teams."

John O'Leary, #1 National Best-Selling author of *On Fire*.

"...I couldn't put it down. It is inspiring and insightful, and every one of us can learn from its valuable lessons."

"I just finished reading Positive Culture Wins. I thought I would read it over the next several weeks but instead, I have read every word of it because I couldn't put it down. It is inspiring and insightful, and every one of us can learn from its valuable lessons."

Ken Theroff, President/CEO Jefferson Bank of Missouri

"...The story format captures the reader to keep turning the pages. I highly recommend you read this book..."

"WOW! This book captures the essence of creating culture not only in your company but in your life. The story format captures the reader to keep turning the pages. I highly recommend you read this book. You will find new ways you can improve and realize you can create The High Achiever Mindset in your daily life."

Eric Lofholm, Eric Lofholm International

"...Creating a culture in your business and life is the roadmap for success and this book will give you the directions to get started."

"Gary has been a friend of Special Olympics MO since 1991. He has shared his talents with the readers in this book on how Special Olympics has impacted not only his life but the impact of his organizations through involvement with his team. Creating a culture in your business and life is the roadmap for success and this book will give you the directions to get started."

Mark Musso, President/CEO Special Olympics Missouri

"...he shows you exactly what it takes to think and act like a high achiever, ultimately resulting in a more effective way to live life."

"Mindset is key to being a present and effective employee, boss, manager, and owner. Gary nails the high achiever mindset in this book and shows you exactly what it takes to think and act like a high achiever, ultimately resulting in a more effective way to live life!"

Matt Ward, Breakthrough-Champion

"...The concepts and ideas are not just for my leadership team, but for every team member. Through the story of "Johnny", I learned the importance of a transparent culture and its profound effects on building a true team..."

After reading Positive Culture Wins, and as I close one business to focus on the growth of another, this book helped me make sure the new company is established correctly. The concepts and ideas are not just for my leadership team, but for every team member. Through the story of "Johnny", I learned the importance of a transparent culture and it's profound effects on building a true team.

Rick Fessler, H&M Holdings, Inc.

"...His approach ensures that readers will not only be engaged but will actually *learn and implement* the valuable lessons he shares about success in life and work."

"In Positive Culture Wins, Gary Wilbers has deftly woven a story that illustrates the key elements of creating a work environment geared for high achievement. His approach ensures that readers will not only be engaged but will actually learn and implement the valuable lessons he shares about success in life and work."

Jeff Cobb, author of *Leading the Learning Revolution* & *Shift Ed*

"...Gary's years of success in building culture within his own businesses shines through the pages of this easy read."

"Culture is at the crux of every successful business. This business fable pushes the reader to think about their own experiences with positive and negative cultures, while examining how a business guided by mission and principles sets the foundation for success in all aspects of a business. Gary's years of success in building culture within his own businesses shines through the pages of this easy read."

Andy Stuckenschneider, IWDG

"...It takes the guesswork out of how to improve your life..."

"Goals are the headlights to knowing where we are going, and this book is the driver and limousine. It takes the guesswork out of how to improve your life today."

Matthew Luadzers, Central Missouri Gogiro

DEDICATION

This book is dedicated to

All my friends at Special Olympics MO whom I have had the pleasure of getting to know since 1994. I have learned so much from the athletes who live life to the fullest no matter what. You show the emotion of love with open arms. You are my inspiration.

My children Chris, Adam, and Elle. I hope this book inspires you to make your life what you want it to be. Remember: Always serve others and you will find your true life's purpose.

Even though this book is a business fable, it has many parallels to my life and to many people who helped me become the person I am today.

This book is written for
You, the reader. As we live our life, we realize the challenges we face each day. I hope this book inspires you to create the life you want.

ACKNOWLEDGMENTS

I am deeply grateful to Michael, Melissa, Ben, and Peggy who made my dream of writing a business fable become a reality. I want each of you to know how much I appreciate your effort and time.

Michael Sahno, you were a great resource who took my concepts and stories and helped me create a first-class business fable. We started our relationship by connecting through LinkedIn. You are not only a writing resource but also a true friend. Thank you for turning my crazy ideas into a book that allows readers to find themselves a part of the story.

Melissa, you finalized the book to a completed product and have been instrumental with the publication. Thank you for helping me complete this dream. You are an amazing person and a great asset to our company.

Ben, you created the success I dreamed of through your insights and understanding about the promotion of this book. You have a bright future; go out and create it.

Peggy, you have inspired me to succeed in life ever since I was in your high school English class. I appreciate your editing of this book. Your friendship and mentorship have been true blessings in my life.

THANK YOU FOR MAKING A DIFFERENCE

Since 1994, I have been associated with Special Olympics Missouri and have learned many life lessons from the athletes. In an effort to help them continue with their quest to become the best they can be, I will be donating $1 from each sale of *Positive Culture Wins* to Special Olympics MO. Thank you for making this possible through your purchase.

I can remember the first summer games I attended in 1994. They were being held on the base of Fort Leonard Wood in Missouri. The opening ceremonies were celebrated with each unit of the military cheering for the athletes as they paraded into the stadium. I remember the hair on my arms sticking up because it was so inspirational. In that moment I became a fan for life and supporter of Special Olympics. Since that night I have had the pleasure of getting to know many of the athletes who participate in Special Olympics. They overcome many challenges and break down barriers every day. I have had the pleasure of volunteering at statewide games, diving in freezing water at their annual

Polar Plunge, and rappelling off a building to support the athletes. Getting our business involved with the financial support of Special Olympics and having our employees volunteer at the games have become very rewarding experiences. I have also had the privilege of serving on the Statewide board and the honor of chairing the Capital Campaign for the Training for Life campus currently being built in Jefferson City, MO.

If you are interested in learning how you or your company can get involved, please check with your statewide Special Olympics. In Missouri you can go to **www.somo.org** or call the statewide office (573) 635-1660.

Be a FAN!

Thank you.

Gary Wilbers

INTRODUCTION

Johnny has a beautiful wife, great kids, a successful career, and a serious problem. He struggles with work, family, and his health. Estranged from his wife and worried about the job he's about to start as Director of Sales with NCI Systems, Johnny is a man on the edge of disaster.

Fortunately, Johnny's new position finds him entering the most positive work environment he's ever experienced. Under the guidance of a well-loved coach, he learns The High Achiever Mindset, the basis of the company's culture. Johnny finds out firsthand that *Positive Culture Wins*.

Filled with practical strategies and an action plan for readers at every level, *Positive Culture Wins* is about changing lives for the better.

TABLE OF CONTENTS

1	A Life of Success	1
2	First Impressions	5
3	The Team	12
4	Meeting The President	20
5	Culture Shock	25
6	Moments of Magic	37
7	The Coach	50
8	Family Ties	63
9	Charge	74
10	A Positive Culture	87
11	Creating Energy	104
12	Family Time	115
13	Making Connections	119
14	Summer Games	134
15	The Struggle	144
16	Influencing Others	150
17	Integration Begins	163
18	Putting It All Together	171
19	The Future	179
20	Putting The High Achiever Mindset To Work	184

1

A LIFE OF SUCCESS?

On a bright, crisp fall day, Johnny and his family loaded up their mini-van to head to their new home in the Midwest. He had taken a job as Director of Sales with Network Cloud Infrastructure (NCI) Systems, a growing technology company.

It was the perfect opportunity for Johnny to leave behind the big-city life and a job he had grown to hate. The only question was how much of his old life would Johnny carry into the new one.

When he graduated from college, Johnny's dream job was to work for a major corporation and move up the ladder to success. He married, and he and his wife Amy began having children.

Over a period of fifteen years, he'd been promoted and moved his family five times across the United States. However, now Johnny's health and his relationship with Amy were both suffering. Their three children – Jack, eight; Billy, six; and Marie, four – were growing up without him. They'd hardly noticed that in recent years he'd been leaving on Sunday afternoons and returning home late Friday night or early Saturday morning, crisscrossing the country for work.

For the last three years Amy pleaded with him to give up the rat race and money for a simpler life.

Johnny wasn't hearing the message. He told himself he enjoyed the art of sales and the accolades that came with his success, but he wasn't happy and neither were Amy and the kids.

"My wife is able to stay home with our children," he justified to himself. "My salary allows us to live in an upscale neighborhood with a gated community. At least they're getting one parent."

The truth was Johnny had a loving wife, beautiful children, a magnificent home in the "right" part of town, and a management job. He knew these were all blessings, but they felt more like a trap: a mortgage, a job he had to keep, a wife and kids who needed him to take care of them and maintain that lifestyle.

Finally, the message came through one night when Amy said, "I'd live in a two-bedroom shack if I could just have more time with you and the kids. All of us together as a family."

Johnny saw the tears in Amy's eyes, and his heart sank. Something had to change.

2

FIRST IMPRESSIONS

On the first day of his new job as Director of Sales, overseeing a team of ten salespeople covering the U.S., Johnny became NCI Systems fifty-first employee. He walked into the office at 7:45 A.M. and was greeted by the Human Resource/Training Director, Tom, who was about six feet tall with a stocky build and a short grey buzz cut.

He said, "Welcome to NCI Systems. Do you go by John or Johnny?"

"I go by Johnny. I'm not sure why, but my Grandpa Joe used to always call me Johnny, and it seems my whole family picked up on it. I guess I liked it. In high school and college, I used to correct my teachers if they called me John."

"Well, then Johnny it is," said Tom. "Johnny, I'm going to give you a tour of the company and introduce you to our family. After that, we'll finish all your necessary paperwork, review our team member manual, and then Charlie will join us for lunch."

Johnny caught his breath. He knew that Charlie was the president of NCI Systems. His first day and he'd be having lunch with the president?

Tom was still speaking, "In the afternoon you'll be spending time with Charlie to review your position, expectations, and our company's Mission, Vision, and Goals."

So that was that. The Director of Sales had direct access to Charlie from day one. It all sounded good, but Johnny remembered how tense meetings had been with the president of his last company and tried not to frown.

As they walked down the hallway, he remembered the worst meeting he had ever had at his old company. With dreadful clarity he recalled specific moments:

"We're restructuring the whole sales department," the president had said breezily. Johnny's blood had frozen. That was his department, and this was the first he'd heard of it.

"When was this decided?" he asked.

The president wheeled on him with pure condescension. "Pretty sure I told you last week."

"No sir, you did not."

"Well, I'm telling you now. We're getting rid of some deadweight and injecting new blood."

"Sir?"

"Salesmen are a dime a dozen, Johnny-boy. Don't worry about it."

Moments later a woman named Marlene raised her hand timidly. "Sir, is it possible to get the minutes of the last meeting from your secretary?"

Again, the president wheeled around in the great leather chair.

"Who are you?"

"M-Marlene S-s-smith, sir."

The president glared and pulled his great bulk from the chair. He towered over her as the room went deathly quiet.

"If I want to hear your voice, I'll ask you a question. You understand?"

"Yes, sir. I'm sorry, sir."

Without warning he exploded, "Don't sorry me, you little twit. Sorry is for losers." He wagged his finger in her face and screamed, "You have something you need, send an email. Now, shut it. Do you hear me?"

Johnny's guts were churning, and he suddenly wondered whether the president was actually going to strike this poor, trembling woman who silently cried as she shook. At last the president, his face nearly purple with rage, sat down. "Where the hell were we?"

Thankfully, Johnny's memory was interrupted as Tom brought him back to the present by introducing him to Mary, a slim blonde woman in a red business suit. Mary's title was Greeting Coordinator.

"Mary is amazing at her position," said Tom, "because she makes the first impression for our entire organization whenever someone calls or visits. Mary, how did your son do in his baseball game last night?"

"Great, Tom. Thanks for asking. He pitched a one-hitter."

"Fantastic! How about Lisa? Is she excited about the upcoming musical she's performing in?"

"Oh, yes," Mary beamed, and Johnny felt the familiar pleasure he took in his own family or rather had taken before he'd gotten so busy working all the time.

Mary said, "If you ever need anything, Johnny, large or small, just let me know. My job is to take care of not only our external guests but also our internal ones."

Johnny said, "Thank you," but wondered about the custom of referring to customers as guests. He was unsure what she meant by internal and external, but there was no time to ponder it. Tom was already moving to the next employees to meet.

3

THE TEAM

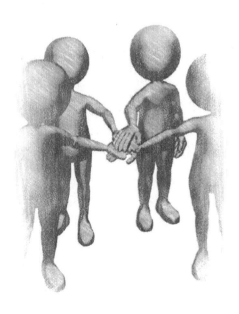

Johnny followed Tom into the Guest Introduction Center where the team in charge of incoming calls and emails from guests worked.

The room was set up in a way Johnny had never seen in corporate America: no offices or cubicles. The team's desks faced each other in a circle with a round table and six chairs in the middle. Sitting in one of these chairs was a tall woman with red hair, Sue Ellen, the Guest Experience Coordinator. Sue Ellen introduced each of her team making sure to point out a positive note about each person's work and one thing about his/her family. She also handed Johnny note cards that she called All-Star cards. Each had a photo of an employee and a personal note about his/her work.

Johnny could see from the delight on

their faces that they liked both the job and supervisor.

Next Johnny and Tom visited the Implementation Team.

"This team is responsible for working with clients to implement our solution into their company," Tom explained as they walked into the room.

Johnny was surprised to see that not everyone in the company looked as perfect and polished as Mary, Sue Ellen, or even Tom. The Implementation Team Coordinator, Eric, was short and pudgy with a shiny bald spot and thick, almost scary-looking eyeglasses. He smiled shyly as Tom and Johnny entered.

"Eric, this is Johnny, our new Director of Sales," Tom said. They shook hands and Tom continued, "Eric has a team of fifteen but only a handful are in today because most of them are already at a client's workplace."

Eric nodded and led Johnny over to a wall covered with pictures of the team. Using these he introduced each team member and added a positive attribute about their work and personal lives.

Johnny was amazed. "How do you remember all this stuff about these employees?" he asked.

With a smile Eric said, "We're family. You don't forget your relatives' names, do you?"

Johnny laughed and felt himself redden. "No," he said. "No, I guess I don't."

Eric introduced Johnny to the other three people who were in the office that day. He explained how the Implementation Team worked hand-in-hand with the Sales Team to deliver what the company promised.

"Johnny, you've heard the motto: 'Over deliver on the promises we make'."

"Sure," Johnny said.

"Well, we've changed that to 'We over deliver in each guest interaction to create loyalty from our clients, team members, and suppliers'."

Eric then showed Johnny a scoreboard that displayed the vital metrics about how his team provided great guest interaction daily, weekly, monthly, and annually.

As they walked back out into the hallway, Tom said, "Next we're going to visit our Strategic Vision Team."

This team consisted of Tom's group of three people referred to as the Human Capital. Tom introduced Johnny to his associates Dave and Kenneth and again mentioned both the quality of their work and a personal attribute that made each of them smile.

So far it all seemed too good to be true, but when Johnny heard the words *human capital*, his thoughts went straight back to his old job: Everyone there was just a tool to be used. It was classic corporate America. We weren't human beings to them; we were human resources, personnel, and pawns. Maybe this place is something like that after all. His heart beat a little faster, and anxiety began to mount in his chest.

There wasn't time to think too much about it because Tom was already taking Johnny to meet his own assistant, Susan, a woman in her late 30s with light brown hair and a warm smile.

Tom greeted her with a friendly, "Morning, Susan. This is Johnny, our new Director of Sales. Johnny, this is Susan."

"Pleased to meet you."

"Susan is the assistant who helps provide support for the Sales Team," Tom continued. "As you know, this is the team you will oversee and grow. The company has expanded its sales and territory over the last several years, and we intend to continue.

"Susan is the oil that allows the engine of this team to run smoothly," added Tom. "She has three children at home, and they're – let's see if I have this right – eight, ten, and fourteen now. Do I have that right?"

Susan beamed, "You sure do, Tom."

"And how is Curt was doing in school?"

Again, Susan smiled. "Every day is an adventure with Curt, but he loves his school," she said to Tom. "Ever since we met Mrs. Jones, Curt has really made progress."

She turned to address Johnny. "Curt has Down syndrome and needed special education to further his development," she explained.

"I'm sorry," said Johnny, leaning in sympathetically.

Susan smiled. "Curt is our gift from God. He has taught me more in his ten years of living than I knew the entire twenty-eight years before he was born."

Tom said, "Susan will introduce you to the rest of your team later and give you the background for your areas of responsibility. As we discussed in your interview, this area is growing and will be the number one reason we achieve our goals as a company as we continue to find, retain, and attract top-level talent. Meanwhile, we're going to see Charlie."

4

MEETING THE PRESIDENT

As Tom walked Johnny to the president's office, he said, "Johnny, when you meet Charlie, he's going to share with you the philosophy he has not only for the company but also for life. Charlie is going to share what he calls his 'High Achiever Mindset'. Make sure you pay attention and take good notes. His assistant, Cindy, will provide you with a journal and a pen. You'll be with Charlie until lunch, and then we'll all meet back here at noon and go to lunch together."

Johnny paused. For the last few years he had always tried to get away from the stress of the office at lunchtime by eating alone in a restaurant or even brown-bagging it when he wanted to save a couple dollars.

"Okay," he said. But he wasn't so sure it was okay. Would he be stuck with all these friendly, cheery people all day, every day? Was lunch together going to be a mandatory thing?

Arriving at Charlie's office, Tom introduced Johnny to Charlie's assistant Cindy. Just as with the other employees, Tom complimented Cindy by referring to some information she had sent to him the previous week about a project.

"That was tremendously helpful," said Tom. "Thanks again."

"My pleasure," Cindy said. She turned to Johnny and, as promised, handed him not only a journal but also a pencil, a pen, and a yellow highlighter. "Take good notes about what Charlie teaches you today," she said. "If you implement his High Achiever Mindset into your daily routine, it will change your life."

Before Johnny had a chance to ask Cindy what she meant, out walked Charlie. He shook Johnny's hand firmly and with a genuine enthusiasm that took Johnny by surprise.

"Johnny, welcome to the team," he said. "We are so excited that you have joined our company!"

Johnny smiled and said, "Thank you, thank you," but in the back of his mind he couldn't help but wonder if this was all sincere. It just seemed way too much.

"If it sounds too good to be true, it probably is," his mother had always told him. Now here he was in what looked and sounded like the best job he'd ever had. But was it for real?

There wasn't any time to think about it, as Charlie was asking questions a mile a minute: "How was the move? Did you have any trouble settling in? And how are your wife and children handling the transition? Remind me of their names again."

Johnny answered each question dutifully until the social hour seemed to be over, and Charlie asked Cindy to bring in some bottled water. Before she left, he made a point of adding, "Johnny, if you ever need anything, either personally or professionally, Cindy can make it happen."

Johnny reflected that this seemed true enough. Cindy had helped arrange his moving process, coordinated all the details of his arrival, and even sent Johnny a list of the best schools in the area.

Charlie thanked Cindy for all her contributions with bringing Johnny aboard, and she left with a radiant smile.

5

CULTURE SHOCK

After Cindy had gone, closing the door softly behind her, Johnny, Charlie and Tom moved into a conference room and sat down at one end of the table together. Charlie sat at the head of the table with Tom and Johnny facing one another.

"Now," said Charlie, "if I know Tom, he has taken you to all the departments that make up our team here at NCI Systems. Right?"

"Yes, sir."

"Well, Johnny, I want to tell you a fact about Tom."

Johnny leaned forward, listening intently.

"Tom has been with this company since day one," said Charlie, "and he's instrumental to our success. Tom's greatest asset, however, is that he is a trusted friend who will help me realize when I am not acting according to the Vision, Mission, Core Values, and Goals we have for this company. Tom, thank you for being a mentor, and I will see you at lunch."

The two men stood up, gave each other a friendly pat on the shoulder, and Tom left. Johnny tried to recall a time he had ever seen two management people be so friendly to each other. He couldn't think of an example.

"Johnny, we are so excited that you have joined our team," Charlie repeated as he sat back down at the table. "I have a question, Johnny. What are your first impressions of our company?"

"Wow! I have to admit, Mr. Jones –"

"I'm sorry, Johnny, but please call me Charlie. You are part of our team now, and I expect all our team members to call me by my first name. Go ahead, please."

"Charlie, I'm not sure where to start. From the time I received the offer to be your Director of Sales, I've been overwhelmed by the generosity of all of you and how I have been welcomed as part of the team.

"The assistance we got – arranging the moving company, helping find a home, walking into our home to a stocked refrigerator, and the welcome video from you and your team – all of it has been truly amazing. Today I showed up for my first day with NCI Systems. I have my own parking space, and Tom welcomed me at the door. I think in the first two hours, I've met everyone in the company and know a little about each one. I also appreciate the All-Star cards with the pictures and some information about each person. It's really quite remarkable."

Charlie beamed. "Well, Johnny, those cards were a suggestion we just implemented from Jack, one of our new team members. He suggested it, and we asked him if he would be willing to take charge of implementing it if we supplied the resources. As you can see, he accepted the challenge. Sorry, please continue."

"Well, I have noticed you have really created a culture for your – our – organization. How did that happen?"

"Before I answer, Johnny, I'd like to ask you: What do you think our culture is here at NCI Systems?"

Johnny hesitated, still feeling anxious. Was it a trick question? But he went ahead and answered in good faith, based on what he'd seen. "I think it's a culture of family with the belief that each person on the team creates a successful company."

Once again Charlie beamed and slapped the table with enthusiasm. "Johnny, that is spot on! Our company culture is focused on each member caring for each individual as though we are family because our actions, our words, and our respect create the environment of trust."

Johnny leaned back nodding. What else could he say? "It struck me how each leader spoke about their team. They always spoke about the attitude each person has toward their work and shared a personal characteristic about each. That was impressive to see."

"Thank you, Johnny. We do that to show respect for each member of the team. It also works to remind us that no one member of our team is more important than any other.

Silently, Johnny nodded in agreement.

"During our time this morning before lunch, I want to share with you our philosophy for NCI Systems, Johnny. I want you to fully understand our Vision, Mission, Core Values, and Goals."

Johnny nodded silently. He felt a growing sense of excitement as if he were about to learn the secret to the company's success.

"These are our Guiding Principles. You must act according to these standards at all times, or you'll be looking for employment elsewhere. This is non-negotiable. We give people time to understand these, but make no mistake, we will terminate based on these principles."

For the first time Johnny felt truly anxious. Could he do it? He'd been in such a negative, toxic environment for so long that he wondered whether it had changed his approach to leading a sales team. Had it changed him?

Charlie was still talking, and there was no time to worry about it now. "Let's first discuss our Vision here at NCI Systems. Our Vision Statement is

---

Success is dependent on taking care of our team members and guests.

As you can see, we put focus on our team first because it's a proven fact that if we take care of the people who work with us, we know and expect they'll take care of our guests, which is what we call our clients."

"I understand," said Johnny.

"Everyone in our organization knows that our company will provide for our team, and we expect everyone on our team to provide for our guests. To make this simple: It is a guiding principle to get to know your team members, each member of their family, and the interests they have outside of the business. Let me give you example: You met Susan, the Assistant to the Sales Team. Tom was having a conversation with Susan and found out Susan's mother had a bad fall last weekend."

"Oh, my goodness," Johnny said quietly.

"Of course, Susan is a team player, so she showed up to work Monday morning with a heavy heart but didn't want to let her team down. As she did every week, she started getting everything lined up for the Sales Team.

"As soon as Tom found out about her mother, Tom and I went to her to express our sadness and ask how we could help. She said that her mother was in the ICU two hours away. We gathered the Sales Team, and Susan instructed everyone what needed to be taken care of that week. I called our pilot to arrange for our corporate jet to fly her to her mother. Cindy, my assistant, set up transportation services for her. Susan was out all last week taking care of her mother. Today is her first day back.

"Now, let me assure you," Charlie continued, "the Sales Team and everyone else in the organization made sure that all our guests were taken care of.

"My first challenge to you is get to know your team members and what makes them who they are. Build relationships with our entire team and our guests, so when they have a problem or issue, they're willing to let you know. You can imagine a different type of company, right? The type where an employee such as Susan wouldn't tell anyone, wouldn't dream of asking for time off because she might lose her position for missing time from work that hadn't been scheduled weeks, or even months, in advance."

"Sure," Johnny said. Imagine it? He'd lived it for many years.

"Remember that our Vision Statement is something we're always striving to reach," Charlie continued, "but no matter what stage we are, we still need to keep working to achieve it.

"Johnny, do you have any questions about NCI Systems' Vision?"

Johnny didn't really know what to say. "Well, it's impressive," he said tentatively. "I mean, I've never had a Vision Statement actually explained to me. I've seen them on the walls of companies. I've even been involved in creating them, but they became statements that were just posted and never really taken into account and followed in the other companies where I have worked."

Charlie nodded. "Well, let me tell you, our Vision Statement is one of our guiding principles in this organization. You'll find that everyone knows it, and every team member is accountable to each other to live it daily.

"Just last week I had one of our leaders question me about a new policy we were planning to implement. She thought it went against our Vision Statement and explained why. We had a discussion with the team and agreed that she was right, so we didn't implement that policy. I publicly acknowledged the leader for living and speaking to our Vision. The next day I took her to lunch to personally thank her for holding our team accountable."

6

MOMENTS OF MAGIC

"Let's discuss our Mission Statement next," Charlie continued. "This Mission Statement is easy to remember, but that doesn't mean it's easy to put into practice day in and day out. The Mission of NCI Systems is

To create moments of magic for our internal and external guests in every interaction.

Now, moments of magic may not be a term you're familiar with. It was coined by Shep Hyken, who is a motivational speaker and now a friend of mine. Shep came here to speak when we probably had ten team members in the company and presented this concept to our team. He wrote about it in *Moments of Magic*, a book we will be asking you to read.

"The concept is that for every interaction we either create a Moment of Magic or a Moment of Misery. Our goal for our internal guests (our team members) and our external guests (clients or customers) is to always create a Moment of Magic. Do you think that if we create magic we'll keep our guests?"

Johnny nodded again in agreement. "Absolutely."

"Have we created some magic since you said yes to working with our company?"

For the first time that day Johnny relaxed into a smile. "I can honestly tell this isn't just some statement you put on the wall. Your company –"

"Excuse me, Johnny. Our company is the right term for you to use from now on."

"Our company lives this statement through the actions we take, what we do, and how we interact each day. Charlie, this helps explain how from the day I accepted the offer to work here, it's been amazing how many Moments of Magic you have created for me and my family."

"Johnny, we see our people as investments in NCI Systems. On average they say it costs $25,000 to $50,000 for every team member you lose in your company. We choose to follow a process we created a year ago called *Success in Hiring*. It's an eight-step framework that allows our success in hiring someone to help us not only recruit great talent but also keep that talent. We'd better continue, or we will miss our lunch appointment. Don't worry; you'll hear more about the *Success in Hiring* program from Tom because we would like to double your current staff over the next six months.

"The Core Values of our company are the foundation for our organization. We want you to base your decision-making on these three Core Values along with our Vision and Mission Statements."

"Okay," said Johnny.

"We'll discuss these in detail," Charlie continued. "Our three Core Values are

Integrity, Character, and Teamwork.

Let's start by defining integrity. Integrity is the quality of being honest and having strong moral principles."

Johnny nodded. "Sure."

"My personal definition is doing the right thing all the time no matter what. Our company was grounded in this core value, and I want you to lead our internal and external guests from this concept."

"Understood," Johnny said.

"Our second core value is character. Character is defined as the mental and moral qualities distinctive to an individual. We understand that each of our team members has their own character at the heart of existence. As long as each person on our team uses character and integrity to guide their decisions, we believe the individual's moral compass is pointed in the right direction."

Johnny nodded silently.

"The last core value of the company brings together the first two to make us a team of individuals working for the greater cause. Our third core value is teamwork. Teamwork is defined as cooperative or coordinated effort on the part of a group of people acting together as a team or in the interests of a common cause. Teamwork is the backbone of this company. I believe that teamwork is the key to success. We have a spirit of cooperation among our team, and if one area needs assistance, we always have others willing to help.

"For the last several months we have been short in the area of responsibility which you will be handling with our Sales Team. Each of our Team Leaders has been helping to make sure the Sales Team can handle our guests to provide Moments of Magic. TEAM stands for Together Everyone Accomplishes More. It's a foundational value of this company.

"Johnny, I know that this is a lot of information to share with you during your first couple of hours with the company, but the main point I want to emphasize is this: If you live by the Vision, Mission, and Core Values of our organization, your success will not only be determined by you but also by your team. That team includes everyone in this organization. Our goal is not to be the biggest company, but to be the best company in our area of expertise, and the best company to work for in this state and even the nation. Specifically, our goals are

1. Designated as one of the Top 10 companies to work for in the state of Missouri by the end of 2019.
2. Become the best company in our industry by the ranking of *Forbes, Entrepreneur*, or *Money by the end of 2020*.
3. Chosen as one of the Top 100 companies in the U.S. to work for in three publications by the end of 2020.

"As you can see, these are the goals we're striving to achieve each day. I'm a firm believer that you must have goals to achieve success in life and business. I had a friend who once told me a quote about goals that I'll never forget: 'Goals: It's like having your headlights on because you know where you are going'."

"As we wrap up our first session, Johnny, what questions do you have?"

"At this point, I'm not sure," he admitted. "But I will say that, as you know, I worked for a rather large company before and never did they share information as you did. I really appreciate this opportunity to work for you."

"Sorry, Johnny, one correction- our company. You're not working for me; you're working for our team. Let's go meet the others for lunch. Everything we discussed is in our *Team Member Success Guide*. We also have online training that covers our Vision, Mission, and Core Values which I want you to view in the next thirty days. Are you hungry?"

"Yes, this has been a great morning!"

Johnny and Charlie met some of the Leadership Team at a locally owned spot nearby called Prison Times, which was located by an old, abandoned prison. It was a sunny day with the temperature in the 70s. As they arrived, everyone at the table greeted Johnny and Charlie. After ordering Tom stood up with a glass of water in his hand.

"Johnny, please stand up."

Aware that he was slightly blushing, Johnny stood.

"As we welcome you to our team today, we want you to know that not only are you a fellow leader of NCI Systems but you are also a trusted friend and mentor to all of us. We are so excited you said yes to joining our company. Cheers! Johnny, would you like to speak?"

Johnny cleared his throat. "Well, first of all, thank you for giving me the opportunity to work for this amazing company. As you know, I have worked for

Fortune 500 Companies, and I've never felt so welcomed and happy to be part of a team. As I learned about the company's Vision, Mission, Core Values and Goals from Charlie this morning, I'm excited to be part of this team. Thank you again for making me feel so welcomed!"

Charlie stood up and asked everyone else to join him. "Please bow your heads. Dear Lord, we come to You today with thankful hearts in bringing a fellow brother to our team. Please bless him and his family as they join the NCI family. Lord, let us realize we do our work for Your purpose. Serving others, as You showed us, is our reward. Let us realize we are sinners, but with Your grace and love we become the people You seek us to be each day. Amen."

Over lunch the leadership team told Johnny the stories of how each person became a member. Charlie talked about how his first two business ventures failed and ended in bankruptcy. Charlie mentioned that this afternoon Johnny would get the opportunity to meet Coach Davis.

"Coach Davis not only saved my marriage of forty-one years, but he's also the reason NCI Systems is the company it is today," said Charlie. "Coach showed me the way to create The High Achiever Mindset in everyone, not only in business but in life too."

As Charlie drove Johnny back to the office from the restaurant, he asked him to be open-minded to the concepts and teachings of Coach Davis.

"Johnny, The High Achiever Mindset is foundational to our success in this company," he said, "but I'll tell you honestly that it's given me even more personally. As Coach shares this wisdom, be sure to correlate the information with both your professional and personal life."

After he parked the car, Charlie told Johnny, "Enjoy your meeting with Coach and I'll see you tomorrow."

Cindy welcomed Johnny back and said she would take him to Coach Davis' office.

7

THE COACH

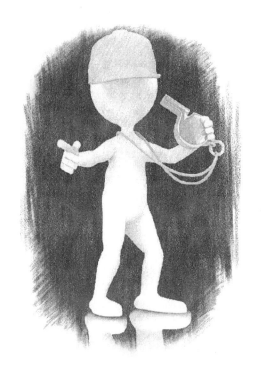

Johnny knocked on the door of Coach Davis' office and a deep, dark voice said, "Come on in." As Johnny entered the room, he saw an older grey-haired man with his back to the door. Coach said, "Have a seat, Johnny."

Johnny circled the desk so he could see Coach's face and sat down. His eyes were focused on the man's face, and before he knew what he was saying, he asked, "Coach, is that you?"

"Yes, Johnny. I am Coach Davis."

Johnny was amazed as he recognized the very same Coach Davis who had been his football coach in high school.

"Coach Davis, I thought you retired from coaching?"

Coach smiled. "Well, Johnny, I retired from coaching high school sports, but Charlie persuaded me to share my coaching and leadership philosophy with his leaders and teammates."

Johnny's head was spinning. "How long have you been here? I mean with NCI Systems?"

"Almost five years. Charlie's business was struggling, and we shared some conversations about what I taught the young men who played football for me. He started using those same philosophies in his business. You know, Johnny, football and life are one and the same because we are on a journey to a destination."

Johnny shook his head in disbelief. He gazed at the wall where Coach Davis had hung pictures of every team that he ever coached. He found 1990, the year he graduated from Valley West, and stood to look closer at the picture.

"Wow, we both had more hair in those days."

Coach Davis chuckled as he watched Johnny walk from picture to picture.

Johnny saw that there were many other photos beyond the Valley West section – signed pictures and autographs from celebrities, famous football players, doctors, and lawyers. Many thanked him for being the best coach and teacher of life.

"You coached all these players?"

"No, but they all crossed my path over the years," said Coach. "Pull up a seat, Johnny."

Johnny sat back down feeling more excited than he had before but still a little confused. How had fate brought him here?

"Tell me, Johnny, why you chose to work for NCI Systems."

Johnny took a breath. It was a relief to talk about it with his old high school coach.

"I've been chasing success for many years, Coach, working for major Fortune 500 companies throughout the U.S. and Canada. I've moved my family five times chasing the American Dream, but my dream became a nightmare. My wife and our kids barely knew who I was."

"How's that?"

"See, I'd fly all over the U.S. and Canada for my career," Johnny said, "and I was gone all the time. I'd usually leave on Sunday and return home late Friday night or early Saturday morning. They barely ever saw me, and when I was there, I wasn't really present. Do you know what I mean?"

"I sure do. Go on."

"Amy pleaded with me over the last three years to give up the rat race. But Coach, I have to admit, I loved what I did. It was just that the travel and hours were killing my health and relationship with my family."

Coach said, "What happened? What was the breaking point?"

Johnny sighed. "Well, finally, on a wintry night last February, I got home late from a sales trip because of flight delays. It was Saturday night when I returned, but I was scheduled to head right back out Sunday morning. I turned my key in the lock and snuck into the house quietly, not wanting to wake my wife or the kids.

"Amy was sometimes a little cold when I came home. I knew she was exhausted and that she was practically raising our children alone. I was the big breadwinner, but I no longer had a relationship with anybody in that house.

"You know how sometimes you walk into a room right after someone has had an argument, and you can feel the tension in the air? That's what it was like walking into our home that night. Amy was sitting at the kitchen table, and the lights downstairs were all on. Something was different.

"Before I even hung up my coat, Amy said, 'I'd live in a two-bedroom shack if I could just have more time with you and the kids. All of us together as a family.' But I didn't really buy that. I wasn't listening. She had the nice house in the gated community and didn't have to work outside the home. What woman would give that up?"

"Coach, I'll admit, I was furious. Wasn't I the one sacrificing for the family? I worked so hard to provide for her and the kids so she could stay home with them. I wish I could say I sat right down and said, 'I'm so sorry, honey. You're right. I haven't been here for you.' But I didn't. I went upstairs and unpacked.

"As I was putting my things away, I came across a picture of you and me at our Senior Football Banquet. I'd never forgotten that talk you gave about success. You said, 'Success is not what you do in life, but the relationships and memories you make with those you love and cherish.'

"Why those words you spoke almost twenty years ago came to me I have no idea. I picked up the phone and called my boss. I left him a voicemail telling him I needed to take the next week off for my family. Long story short, we made a goal that within one year I would find a new job, and we would move within fifty-to-sixty miles from our original hometown."

Coach slapped the desk with one hand his eyes twinkling. "Johnny, welcome home! Has anyone told you my role in our company?"

"No," Johnny said.

"They consider me the Coach of the Coaches at NCI Systems. I always thought that when my days were over in coaching and instructing students, I'd just retire and live the good life of fishing, golf, traveling, and hunting. I retired for all of sixty days and was so bored with it that I knew I needed to find something I enjoyed doing for the rest of my life.

"Well, Charlie is a great friend, and I was having lunch with him one day. We were discussing how we could share the wisdom we have gained over the years with those who were important to us. About a week later Charlie called me over to his office and offered me a part-time role with NCI Systems as a Coaches' Coach for his team. I have been here for five years, and I'm having the time of my life seeing this company grow its people.

"You already know what our Vision Statement is. My role is to help you understand what we term The High Achiever Mindset. We believe that $E + C + I + I = GR$ will translate to success not only professionally but also in your personal life.

Johnny asked, "What does it stand for?"

"Energy + Connections + Influence + Integration = Great Results.

"Let's take a look at this chart."

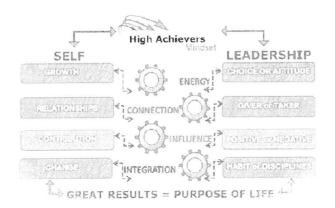

"The first key is to realize that The High Achiever Mindset is based on the four pillars you must put in practice, as you can see in the middle section

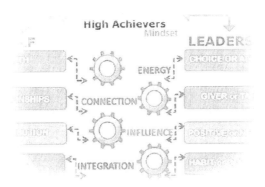

"We'll discuss each one in detail over the next few days," said Coach, "but let's have an overview of the concept today."

"Great."

"You'll notice on the left of the chart it says SELF. On the right of the chart it says LEADERSHIP. In the middle are the keywords for the four pillars – Energy, Connections, Influence and Integration. The High Achiever Mindset rests on the basic principle that you cannot become a High Achiever leader unless you practice these principles first. The key to success is to adopt them for yourself.

"You see there on the chart by the word Energy we have the word Growth. You must be willing to grow first before you can share your leadership with others. I now must ask you a very serious question: Are you willing to learn and grow to become a High Achiever Leader for NCI Systems?"

"Yes," Johnny said. "Of course, I am, Coach."

"I'm going to be challenging you these next several days, and I want you to remember what you just said. This process may seem easy, but it's very challenging. You see, our past experiences will create roadblocks for learning and accepting this new mindset we're asking you to adopt."

Johnny nodded his understanding, but he felt worried inside. Would the Coach push him hard as he had in football practice? Only now it would be his heart and mind tested, not his body. But there was no time to wonder as Coach was still talking.

"Each day we are going to break down the strategy behind each pillar and discuss how first we must change to truly become the leader of High Achievement. I want you to take this playbook home tonight and read it over. Please start by sharing these concepts with your wife."

"Okay." Johnny took the playbook, thinking about Amy. What would she think of all this? Would she even care about The High Achiever Mindset much less the four pillars? Already he could feel his anxiety increasing. He tried to smile as Coach continued.

"I'm looking forward to seeing you grow both in this company and your life. You always were one of my favorites of all the players I coached. Now I get to coach you to become the person God intended you to be. See you tomorrow at nine here at my office." He offered his hand, and Johnny shook it.

"Thanks, Coach. See you tomorrow."

8

FAMILY TIES

Johnny's head was spinning as he left Coach's office. What did he mean by becoming the person God intended me to be? Johnny drove home that night with Coach's words ringing in his head: "The person God intended me to be."

As Johnny opened the front door, all three of the children ran to him and shouted, "Daddy!" Jack and Bill both hugged him while Marie, the four-year-old, threw her arms around his leg and wouldn't let go. Johnny grinned from ear-to-ear.

"How was your first day?" Amy asked as she walked up behind the children.

"Awesome, great, terrific, and mind-boggling."

Amy smiled gently shooing away the children and ruffling Billy's hair in the process. "Now, honey, you'll have to explain that statement."

Johnny just shook his head still thinking about it all.

"This company is absolutely amazing. They made sure I felt like part of the team. I met with every department and leader and was introduced to the entire staff, and that was just this morning. I had lunch with Charlie and the leaders. In the afternoon I met with Coach Davis, my high school football coach who now works for NCI Systems as the coach for their team."

Amy looked confused. "Wait a minute. They have a football coach to coach their employees?"

"I couldn't believe it myself. He was a big influence on me as a young person, and now here he is working for this company. Honey, I hadn't seen him since high school. He shared this playbook with me that I'm supposed to review tonight with you," said Johnny handing her the book.

"With *me*?"

"Yes, maybe after the kids go to bed. He also said that tomorrow we will be discussing The High Achiever Mindset and how we implement these strategies in both professional and personal lives."

Amy nodded solemnly.

"The strangest part was that as we were wrapping up he said that he would coach me to be the person God intended me to be. What do you think he meant by that?"

Amy looked up from the playbook and their eyes met.

"Well, it's not like you have been that faithful with your faith since we have been married. Why don't you take the kids out to the playground before we have dinner? After we put the kids to bed, as you said, we can take a look at the playbook."

Johnny took the book back from her and smiled. The lingering sadness in her eyes told him that he had a long way to go. Suddenly he felt much less positive about what he was getting into than he had while at the office with all the team cheering him on.

Still he knew he had to make a start, and it had to begin here. He kissed Amy on the lips and brushed back a lock of her hair that had fallen down over her forehead.

"Thank you, honey," he said simply. "And thank you for all you do." As he kissed her, he noticed she had arched one eyebrow. She looked somehow hopeful although the expression of concern hadn't faded.

"Last one out to the swing set has to push Daddy," he called out while the giggling kids rushed out to meet him. Amy shook her head and smiled before returning to the kitchen.

Johnny cleaned up the kitchen after dinner while Amy spent some much-needed time with the children. It wasn't until after eight that Johnny finally put their oldest to bed. As he walked back out to the family room, Amy was looking at the playbook.

He sat beside her on the sofa and looked at the book. Amy asked, "Have you reviewed this yet?"

"No, I just got it from Coach at the end of the day."

"Look at this diagram," Amy said and began to read from the playbook:

'The High Achiever Mindset is based on four pillars that set the foundation for your life. Those four pillars are Energy, Connections, Influence, and Integration. When we allow these pillars to work in our everyday lives, we attain great results. Our ultimate goal is not great results but finding the true Purpose of our Life. God wants each of us to be the person he created us to be. The challenge is in our world. Most people chase life's purpose through career, status, or ego.

'The true Purpose of Life is to find and become the person you were intended to be. If we use our Energy to make great Connections, they will Influence us to create Integration to help us solve the puzzle of our Purpose of Life.

'As you read the following pages, please allow this story to help unveil the person you want to become".

"What does unveil the person you want to become mean?"

"I can't say I really know for sure," said Johnny. "But I've got a feeling that I'm about to find out."

That night Johnny fell asleep easily for the first time in months. But in the middle of the night, he had a terrible dream: He could see the fluorescent lights overhead in his old office and smell the cleaning chemicals they used to clean the floors. In the dream he was right in the middle of a disagreement with a co-worker.

"I don't care what you think about this method, Johnny," the man said bearing down on the nickname with heavy sarcasm as if speaking to a child. "That's the way we do it at this company; it's the way we've always done it; and it's the way we're always going to do it!"

Johnny could feel himself reddening as he got angrier and angrier. "Look, Bill," he sputtered, "I'm just trying to offer an alternative way of looking at the problem."

"Listen, Johnny," Bill repeated, again stressing his name sarcastically. "I know what I'm talking about, all right? And I don't have time for any more of this. So if you have a problem with it, take it upstairs." He began shuffling items on his desk as if he were too busy to talk further.

"Okay," Johnny said and with his hands in the air backed out the door into the hallway. "Oh, hey, Lucy. Good morning."

With irritation Lucy glanced up from her purse. She was digging for something as she walked. "What's up, Johnny?" She continued to walk, so he had to speed up to keep pace with her.

"Have you had a chance to read the report from Arnold?"

"Not my department, not my job," she snapped. "I need a cigarette."

She found the pack in her purse and dug further for her lighter.

"I thought everyone had to read it," Johnny said.

"Don't worry about it," Lucy said waving him away with her free hand. "The hell with that fat jerk anyway."

Johnny's guts were churning. "Who? Arnold?"

At last Lucy came to a halt. She leaned closer to Johnny and said, "We're going to kill him. Are you in?"

"What?" His blood ran cold.

"Yeah, Arnold. We're going to kill him."

With a start Johnny lurched forward with sweat on his brow, back, and arms. He was in bed. His breath came in short, sharp bursts, and it took what seemed a long time before he realized it was only a nightmare.

"You okay?" Amy whispered.

"I'm okay. Just a bad dream. Go back to sleep, honey."

"Mm." Amy turned over and sighed falling back to sleep almost immediately while Johnny stared at the ceiling as his head rested on the pillow again.

9

CHARGE

The following morning with the playbook in hand, Johnny returned to the office. He knew he was going to have to talk to Coach Davis and Charlie, and he figured they would be discussing more about The High Achiever Mindset and those four pillars of Energy, Connections, Influence, and Integration.

He felt as if he was in school again, and although he was excited about the new role, he was nervous too. He knew how it worked: You're in your "evaluation period" for the first ninety days, and this was day two.

Charlie's assistant, Cindy, greeted him with a friendly, "Good morning, Johnny."

"Good morning."

"Would you like a water or anything before you meet with the guys?"

"No, thank you. I'm fine," Johnny said.

He had a moment to observe her while she put a couple of file folders into a desk drawer. He figured she was probably in her early 60s. She was mature, the organizer type. She could have been employed at multiple companies throughout her career, but he thought he remembered Charlie saying something about her sticking with him through the years. That probably said something.

"Charlie and Coach Davis are meeting now, but they'll be with you in just a minute," said Cindy.

As Johnny took a seat, she continued, "You know, these last five years of working with Charlie have been the best. He really cares about his people first and the business second."

Johnny smiled. "I'm just amazed to see Coach here; he was my high school football coach many moons ago."

Cindy smiled back. "I know. I'm sure I don't have to tell you this, but make sure you take good notes today. The information they share with you will not only transform your professional career but also work with your family."

Johnny asked, "Charlie has been in business over twenty years, but you mentioned that the last five years have been the best. I thought you were with him from the start?"

"I have been with him since the beginning of several of his businesses," Cindy said, "but he's made some changes in his life, and he was not the same business person he is today. I won't share the complete story because I'm sure Charlie will give you the background, but let's just say, he has made a total transformation in the last five years."

Just then Charlie came out.

"Good morning," he said, his voice as confident as ever.

"Good morning," said Johnny.

"Cindy, thank you for keeping Johnny company." He turned to Johnny. "How was your evening?"

"Great!"

"What does that tell me? Well, not much. Please share with me if you had time to review the playbook we gave you last night?"

"Yes, I reviewed it with my wife Amy," Johnny said. "We were both impressed with the type of company you have here at NCI Systems."

"Sorry, Johnny, just have to remind you: it is WE. This company is because of each person who works here, not MY company but OUR company. I understand it will take some time to get used to, but I believe the language we use makes a difference."

"Got it. Our company."

"I want each one of our team members to know they are the success of OUR team," said Charlie. "I've tried in the past to do it my way, and I'll tell you, I almost lost everything in the process. Let's go in and join Coach Davis, and I'll share more of that story."

As they walked into the office, Coach Davis got up and came over to shake Johnny's hand. The two men said good morning to each other, and all three of them sat down around the conference table.

"I understand Coach Davis was your high school football coach?"

"Yes, he was the best. He always taught us leadership and life lessons as well as football."

"Well," Charlie said, "that's the reason I hired Coach to join our team. Not only is he a trusted friend, but he's also the type of coach I wanted to share our business and life philosophy with our team."

"I understand."

"Did you know that Coach Davis is in the top ten of all the winningest coaches in the state of Missouri? He's going to be inducted into the Missouri Sports Hall of Fame in a few months."

Before Johnny could respond, Coach Davis said, "Thank you, Charlie. But you know this isn't about me. It's about how we can change people's lives. If we are willing to connect with people in business, then we can have them take those lessons and use them in their personal lives. My greatest satisfaction is when I see people not only change themselves but also change their family culture, which is a great transition into our topic today."

He turned from Charlie. "Johnny, today I want to have Charlie explain to you why he believes culture is so important not only for NCI Systems but also in our daily living."

Johnny took his pen and got ready to write in the journal he had brought with him.

Charlie approached a whiteboard and wrote the word CULTURE in bold letters.

CULTURE

He said, "Culture is defined as 'the integrated pattern of human knowledge, belief, and behavior that depends upon the capacity for learning and transmitting knowledge to succeeding generations' in the Merriam-Webster dictionary. Sounds like a mouthful, Johnny. But the key to this definition is that word integrated, which is defined as 'to form, coordinate, or blend into a functioning or unified whole.' So that is the definition, but to me it means: Sharing knowledge to transform our professional and personal lives that permeates each person we interact with in life. Johnny, make sure you write this definition down because this is the foundation this business is built on. If you don't have this foundational cornerstone, you will never succeed here."

Charlie paused a minute and looked out the window. Johnny wrote the definition down and glanced up at Charlie who was obviously deep in thought.

Coach Davis picked up the thread, "Johnny, I have known Charlie many years, and he was always a good businessman. But about six years ago I could tell he wasn't very happy with his life despite whatever successes he'd had."

Charlie chimed in, "Johnny, I was not only unhappy with my business, but I was also failing at my commitments at home. My family didn't enjoy being around me anymore, and I didn't enjoy being around them. I was about to walk away from them because I thought they didn't appreciate what I did for them so they could have all the nice things in their lives."

Johnny thought that sounded familiar.

"Then one day as Coach and I were having lunch, he said something to me that changed my life: 'Your happiness is not based on the things you have, but on the acts of love you give'."

"Frankly, I was stunned. I'd never heard him talk that way, but it hit me hard. Coach asked me to write that statement down and journal about it every day for the next week."

"Well, Johnny, imagine me with a journal! That was not my style, but I took his advice, and for the next week I journaled every day. By the end of that week, I had discovered that it wasn't my business or my family that was the problem. It was *me*.

"For the next year I asked him to coach me to become someone who is willing to give love in all my interactions. Let me tell you, I don't think he ever had a more difficult student than me. I did not know how to do that."

Coach chimed in, "Charlie did have to learn some new strategies because learning is one thing, but as we told you, it's about sharing knowledge to transform your professional and personal lives that permeates each person we interact with in life. It's not a statement but a way we live our lives each day. The key is that we are willing to learn and create habits around real goals every day."

Coach stood up and pulled something from his front pocket. "Johnny, I'd like to give you this armband so you can remember this saying: CHARGE. As you can see, it stands for Create Habits Around Real Goals Everyday.

This is a motto we want you to adopt for life. Are you willing?"

"Yes," said Johnny placing the armband on his wrist.

Coach turned back to the president. "Charlie, why don't you share some of the background of your research about culture and tell Johnny about some of your failures along the way so he understands why this is now your life's mission?"

10

A POSITIVE CULTURE

Charlie stood in front of the whiteboard and wrote the following NCI Systems Culture Statement:

Guiding your ascension in business and life.

"Johnny," said Charlie, "I have done a lot of research on culture and have created some failures in the cultures of my companies over the years. Probably you had a few job situations in toxic workplace environments, right?"

Johnny hesitated. "We-ell…"

"It's all right," Charlie went on. "I know it's bad form to say anything negative about a former employer, especially if it's your most recent one. But let me ask you this: How many places have you worked where you frequently heard people make statements such as these:

By the time Charlie finished, Coach and Johnny were both chuckling.

"All of them," said Johnny, and Charlie and Coach both said, "Exactly!" at the same time.

"Johnny, I was very lucky," Charlie went on. "I had multiple businesses at one time and over a hundred and fifty employees. But I have to admit, I thought the reason for my success was because I was such a great businessman. I want you to understand where I come from so you know why I believe our culture is so critical to this company.

"I started my businesses at a young age and worked long hours. The more successful I became, the more I wanted. I realize now that I was like a kid on one of those merry-go-rounds: I couldn't ever get off. The problem was that I was always trying to speed up the merry-go-round, so I worked my people more. I never appreciated what they did to make the organizations successful. I expected them to work long hours, and if I caught someone slacking off, I would fire them on the spot!

"Then nine years ago as the economy changed, two of my largest businesses failed. We had to declare bankruptcy in those companies which really hit me hard financially. But the stories I heard about some of my staff losing what they had because they weren't prepared for not having a job really crushed me personally. Thanks to

Coach I realized it was time to change. We started NCI on a shoestring and a prayer. Yes, it is amazing how you lean on your faith in time of trouble, but we take it for granted when things are going great."

"Sure," said Johnny.

"Let me tell you about my own failures," said Charlie. "As I said, before I had talked with Coach, I was unhappy in business, and I was failing in my family life. I started several businesses and ran them into the ground. I started another business, and it was successful financially. I had learned from some of my past mistakes, but I was still miserable.

"My family hardly ever saw me, and when they did, I was in a bad mood. I had gained weight and was out of shape to the point where I always took the elevator instead of the stairs, even for just one floor. My business was making money, but I was working eighteen hours a day, and my staff hated me. I mean hated. Even Cindy out there."

Johnny stopped smiling. "Really?"

"Oh yes. I knew that she was miserable working for me just as I was miserable running that company. She didn't say much then but ask her now, and she'll confirm what I'm telling you. I was always right. It was my way or the highway. My people were scared and didn't respect me, and I was fine with that. I wanted to be feared. Everyone in that place was demoralized, stressed out, burned out, and any other kind of out you can think of. A few of them were on their way out the door, thrilled to get jobs somewhere else. The human resources department was a revolving door."

"What happened?"

"Well, I'd been through a couple of bankruptcies by then, and I didn't want to have that happen again. I was frightened of the prospect of the company going under, so I decided to cash out while I could. I sold it and started NCI Systems with just a handful of people from the old company.

"When I started NCI Systems, I was still in the same mindset only now I had more money in the bank. I was feeling financially more secure but still miserable in every way. I could see that there was a good chance I would have the same problems with the new company that I'd always had, and I didn't want to keep repeating the same pattern, but I also didn't know what to do differently. I thought it was somehow everybody else's fault. I didn't know that the problem rested with me.

"Then Coach and I had that lunch and he told me 'Your happiness is not based on the things you have but on the acts of love you give.' And the rest, as they say, is history.

"As I researched and learned strategies from Coach, I realized that attitude plays a large role in how we approach life. Coach always quotes Charles Swindoll, 'Life is 10% what happens to you and 90% how you react to it.' Isn't that right, Coach?"

"You got it, Charlie," said Coach.

"I knew I wanted to change how I did business," Charlie went on, "because I still carried a lot of regret and grief over my former staff who I had lost when those businesses went bankrupt."

Coach stood back up and added, "Johnny, I want you to know that Charlie has learned his lesson the hard way, but he has done everything possible to help his former staff recover from that challenge. Charlie visited every employee and apologized in person to them and their families except for five individuals who wouldn't agree to meet with him because they're unwilling to forgive. He now has created a foundation for these families, and NCI families as well, that awards scholarships to help them attend college.

"So, yes, Charlie has moved forward by understanding that we are forgiven if we are willing to forgive. Some of those former employees are now part of the NCI team. Charlie, you're a good man and a servant leader because of the actions you have taken since the bankruptcy."

Charlie stood back up as Coach sat down. "Thank you, Coach, I appreciate your kind words. One of my favorite Bible quotes is Proverbs 29:18: 'Where there is no vision, the people will perish.' I had to learn this the hard way, but I now realize your vision will drive the culture you want to achieve both in business and in life. This is why I believe culture is our focus here at NCI."

With that he tapped the whiteboard. "Our NCI Systems Culture Statement is Guiding your ascension in business and life. To me ascension means helping others rise to a higher level, not only in business but also in their personal lives. I want you to know the company cannot do it for you. It takes both of us working together to help you reach a higher level."

Charlie wrote Climber and Stuck.

"The High Achiever Mindset starts with understanding the difference between a climber mindset and a stuck mindset," said Charlie. "If you look up the word ascend, you'll see it means either to go up, climb, or rise. A climber mindset means you're always working to move forward, or, even better, upward. Onward and upward, they always say, right?"

"Sure," said Johnny.

"And if you have a climber mindset, you keep going. Even if you fail at something, you can learn how to avoid making the same mistake again.

"Of course, the stuck mindset is the opposite: make the same mistakes over and over again, complain, whine, play it safe, complain some more, and repeat. We all know about that one, right?"

"Right."

"Okay," said Charlie, "enough about that. And you know, you can try to be a climber and still get stuck a lot. Do you know what I mean?"

Do I ever, thought Johnny. But instead he merely said, "I think so."

"Johnny, did you know I called every one of your references, and they all said great things about you, but there was one piece of disturbing information when I asked about your family? Do you know what that was?"

Johnny cleared his throat. "Yes, that I was headed for a divorce if I didn't make some changes."

"Yes, Johnny, your references mentioned that in one way or another. I know you have the capability to lead our sales team, but you must realize you have some work to do to start leading your family again."

"Yes, I understand, Charlie. After speaking with Coach yesterday, it became very evident."

"Great. I also want you to know that Coach Davis told me what a great individual you were, not only in playing football but the effort you put forth to learn what he was teaching you in high school. It was easy to bring you here to help you find your purpose in your life.

"Johnny, I have another meeting I need to attend, so I'm going to wrap up our discussion today. Coach will finish up with you, and I'll see you both at lunch."

As Charlie headed for the door, Johnny asked, "Charlie, do you have a minute?"

"Sure, Johnny. What's up?"

"I want you to know how much I appreciate the opportunity to work for you, I mean for our company. I promise I will not let you down."

"Thanks, Johnny, but don't worry about letting me down. Don't let those closest to you down, meaning your family and now your family at NCI." Charlie closed the door behind him.

Tears sprang to Johnny's eyes, and Coach must have seen this as he handed him a tissue. Coach asked, "What do you think of Charlie?"

"I have never had multiple conversations with the owner of the company in the first two days on the job. The care and love he has shown me has already blown me away. I'll be honest. It's hard to take in because in my previous jobs they no more cared about me than the man in the moon. It was all about hitting our quarterly numbers so my bosses would get their bonus checks."

"You have quite an opportunity here to become the person God means for you to be."

Johnny looked up at him. "I told Amy you said that yesterday, and I'd like to ask you a question about it."

"Sure, what's that?"

"What do you mean the person God means for me to be?"

"Great question, Johnny. I believe God has a plan for us even before we are born. However, he gave us free will, and that gets in our way. We think we know what's best for us, and we start to put our faith on hold."

"My wife said something to me about that last night," Johnny said. "She said, 'It's not like you have been that faithful with your faith since we have been married.' I have to admit, it hurt my feelings a bit."

"Well, some people stop attending church services; some go but they are never present, and some just go through the motions," Coach said. "It doesn't matter where you are today, it matters if you're willing to start allowing God into your personal and business life. God is not meant to be available to us just when we need him but at all times. I want you to start journaling every evening before you go to bed and ask yourself this question: God, what are you calling me to become in my life? Make sure you write at least one paragraph every evening. Can you do that?"

Johnny hesitated. "Yes, but what if nothing comes for me to write about?"

"Don't worry, God will take care of that part. See how we want to control the process? Just be open and let God speak to you.

"Johnny, it's only an hour until lunch, and I have to meet with one of the other team members. Why don't you spend some time with your team and get to know them? In your playbook we have copies of a sheet that covers *What You Need to Know About Your Team*."

Johnny flipped to the page as Coach pointed it out, and their eyes met again when Johnny saw that the page was blank.

"Understand that it's blank because you have to visit with them to get the information. Don't worry. They know you'll be asking them questions. My only suggestion is don't just ask questions but follow up and really be present with them so you get to know who they are. Make sure you meet me at the front desk at ten to twelve so we can ride together."

"Great, thanks, Coach."

Coach turned around and said, "My pleasure. I am so happy you are part of our team."

11

CREATING ENERGY

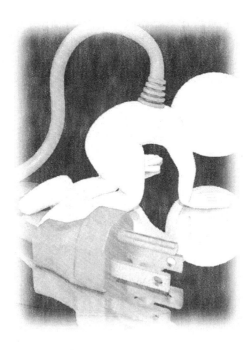

After lunch Johnny met back up with Charlie and Coach Davis.

"So, Johnny, let's talk about energy," said Coach. "Energy helps us look at our purpose and determines why it is important to our mindset. Energy is a choice we make daily that impacts our purpose in all aspects of life from work to marriage and family life. You're here at NCI Systems in a new job, so you have made a choice to be energetic and productive today.

"Let's look at your attitude in general. If you fill a glass with water halfway, do you see the glass as half empty or half full?"

Johnny hesitated. He knew the better answer would be to say half full, but he had to be honest and admit that he oftentimes looked at it as half empty, especially lately with being gone such long hours and the stress at home. At last he admitted, "Sometimes I do see it as half empty, I'm sorry to say."

"You're not alone, Johnny," said Coach. "Remember: Energy is all about the growth you want in your life in two areas: exercise and productivity."

Johnny glanced down at his midsection. He'd been going to the drive-through at fast food restaurants so often in recent years. He regretted the way it made him feel and look.

"Your weight probably isn't exactly where you want it anymore," Coach said. "Is that right?"

"It's true," said Johnny. "Too much fast food, not enough exercise. I feel the difference." In the back of his mind, though, he began to feel a bit defensive. It was one thing to talk about this in a private conversation with Coach, but to talk about it in front of the company president seemed inappropriate. Was it really any of their business if he was a little overweight?

Before he could think about it more, Coach continued on.

"Johnny, your leadership mindset will definitely be much more solid when you exercise regularly. Exercise is the fuel that energizes us. We encourage everyone on the team to take better care of themselves than they did before they started with us. Do you know that over sixty percent of the population is now considered overweight and over thirty percent of adults are obese? It's an epidemic.

"I'm going to give you a list you can take home with you. These are simple steps you can easily implement to increase your overall energy level in three areas: physical, nutritional, and what I call daily boosts. These range from creating daily peak productivity times to making sure you get enough sleep to meditating. There are fifteen suggestions, five in each category."

"I promise you that if you implement one of these energy boosters from each category in the next ninety days, you will see your energy level increase. Implement two from each category, and you will see a total energy transformation. Your willingness to implement these becomes your first leadership test."

Johnny looked down at the list and saw the following:

PHYSICAL APPROACH

1. 7-9 HOURS SLEEP
2. CARDIO WORKOUT 3-5 TIMES/WEEK
3. WALK OUTSIDE EVERYDAY FOR A MIN. OF 30 MINS.
4. DEEP BREATHING EXERCISES 3 TIMES/DAY
5. MEDITATE OR TAKE ALONE TIME DAILY

NUTRITIONAL APPROACH

1. DRINK ½ BODY WEIGHT IN OUNCES OF WATER DAILY
2. TAKE A MULTI-VITAMIN, VITAMIN D, & OMEGA 3
3. DON'T DIET! CHANGE YOUR EATING HABITS
4. START THE DAY WITH A HEALTHY BREAKFAST OR SHAKE
5. MINIMIZE ALCOHOL, CAFFEINE, & SUGAR

DAILY BOOSTS

1. BE COMPLETELY PRESENT DURING CONVERSATIONS
2. MAKE EVERYONE YOU INTERACT WITH SMILE OR LAUGH
3. DO A SIMPLE ACT OF KINDNESS
4. IF YOU HAVE A SEDENTARY JOB, TAKE 3-4 MINS. TO GET UP & MOVE EVERY HOUR
5. TAKE A LUNCH BREAK AWAY FROM YOUR DESK

Yikes, he thought.

He looked back up as Coach continued, "I suggest you take a look at each of these three areas. Which ones are you already doing? Decide which one from each list you'll start doing today."

"Okay," said Johnny.

"Remember," Coach said, "the key is accountability. We don't set our team members up to fail, so we're going to help you get started on making some of these positive changes. These will make you feel better, but my saying that doesn't get you feeling as if you want to do them. Your accountability partner will help ensure your success."

"Accountability partner?"

Coach chuckled, and Charlie sat back and smiled. "Yep," said Charlie, pressing a button on his phone. "Eric, can you come back here when you have a moment?"

"Be right there, Charlie," came a voice over the phone.

Johnny caught his breath. He had just met Eric yesterday and couldn't quite place him in his mind after meeting so many team leaders and staff. But it all made sense when the door opened and in walked Eric.

Immediately Johnny remembered that Eric was the Implementation Team Coordinator. Eric was about his age, short and pudgy, with a shiny bald spot and thick glasses. To Johnny he looked like the classic computer geek you'd expect to be in charge of something in a tech startup such as NCI Systems.

"You remember Johnny, our new Sales Director," said Coach. "He just started yesterday."

"Nice to see you again," Eric said, shaking Johnny's hand.

"Likewise."

Coach said, "Eric, meet your new accountability partner." He turned to Johnny. "Johnny, Eric struggled with his weight for years before joining us here. Tell Johnny how much weight you've lost since you started here."

"Sixty-five pounds," Eric said.

Johnny whistled. "Wow," he said. "Congratulations."

"Thank you."

"Eric is doing great," Coach continued, "but he hasn't reached his ideal weight yet. How many more pounds you figure?"

Eric patted his belly. "I think I'd be happy with another twenty-five to thirty."

"There you go," said Coach. "You know, our leadership is tested every day by the attitudes we show. We all get excited about starting something new, but the challenge is to finish the job. Thanks, Eric," he said, and Eric headed back out the door.

"Thanks, Eric," Johnny called after him.

Coach continued, "Now, Johnny, the second part of energy is in the area of productivity. Energy, not time, is the fundamental currency of high performance. The hours in our days are fixed, but the quantity and quality of available energy is not. It is our most precious resource. The more we take responsibility for the energy we bring to the world, the more empowered and productive we actually are. Small changes in your behavior alter how productive you are. It all starts with having a climber mindset. Your mindset always comes first.

"As a coach, my goal is to give you guidance about how you can become an inspiring, influential leader in your professional and personal life, just as I've done with everyone on the team, starting with Charlie. Based on my track record, do you think I can do the same with you?"

Johnny nodded. "Absolutely, Coach."

"We want you to come right out of the gate with a win. So the first challenge you have is to decide what strategies you will implement in the next twenty-four hours. We have seven key strategies that will help you stay focused."

Coach wrote on the whiteboard:

1. AVOID EXAGGERATIONS AND NEGATIVES.
2. IMMEDIATELY STOP NEGATIVE ENERGY.
3. FOCUS ON THE POSITIVE.
4. REALIZE IT IS OKAY TO MAKE MISTAKES.
5. MIX WITH POSITIVE PEOPLE.
6. BE GRATEFUL.
7. FOCUS ON THE PRESENT.

When he had finished writing, Coach turned around and read each of the strategies aloud. Then looking Johnny in the eye, he said, "Energy is the fuel for your life. We have to create the climber mindset for growth and demonstrate our leadership through our choices and attitude. Is it always easy? No. But it is simple.

"Here's a card for you to keep with you at all times. We have also included this in your playbook under the Energy section.

"I'm going to give you an exercise, and I want you to take it home and work on it tonight. It's in your playbook. List ten things about your life that are not optimum right now. They could be related to your health, your work mindset, and your personal relationships. Those are some possibilities. Try to come up with at least ten. That's Column A.

"In Column B write some possible solutions for these problems. Make sure you come up with at least one, preferably more, solutions for each. If one doesn't work, maybe a different solution will. You got it?"

"I got it, Coach."

12

FAMILY TIME

That night Johnny arrived home to find Amy and the kids ready to eat and sitting around the table waiting for him. It was like a scene in an old iconic Norman Rockwell painting. His timing was perfect. Amy had just finished making dinner, and the only thing missing was him. Now here he was, and there were smiles all around as they began their meal together. Johnny felt the warmth of his familiar family experience finally starting to come back again. He was home.

When the dishes were put away and it was time to work on the assignment from Coach, Johnny struggled mightily. He knew what to put in Column A – his weight gain, his still-just-barely-warm- relationship with the family, and his worries about the future. But solutions? He was fresh out of those. All he could think of were the little gems of positivity he'd been getting from work, but he couldn't see how to use them specifically to solve his problems.

He looked at the seven key strategies he'd written down that Coach had put on the big board. Immediately stop negative energy caught his eye. When was the last time he had done that? He thought back to the conversation about exercise, and told Amy he was going out for a quick walk.

"A walk? Where?" She looked confused and concerned.

"Just around the block. Want to come with me?"

"But the kids?"

He grinned. "Bring 'em along."

Once outside it quickly became clear to Johnny that this was not going to be serious exercise. The kids ran around having a great time with the novelty of going out with their parents for nothing more than a walk. Amy or

Johnny had to keep reining them in. They stopped half a dozen times over the next thirty minutes. But it was fun, and it was family. Johnny was happy, and so were Amy and the kids.

When they returned, he picked up the paper and looked at Column B again. Much to his surprise Johnny quickly came up with one idea after another. He wrote them down as quickly as he could without regard to whether he thought they were any good. Before long he was finished. He had two or even three potential solutions for every item in Column A. With a sense of satisfaction, he put the work away and spent some quiet time with Amy. He felt that he might really be onto something here.

13

MAKING CONNECTIONS

The following morning Johnny met with Coach again. Charlie had meetings all day, so it looked as though it was going to be just Coach and Johnny at first.

"Johnny, how did it go last night with the exercise I gave you?"

Johnny handed it over with pride. "You know, it's funny. When I first started working on this at home, I had a really hard time. I just couldn't think of anything. Then I decided to take one of your basic suggestions and get some physical exercise. Amy and the kids came with me on a walk around our block, and when we got back, the ideas just flowed. It was like that little bit of exercise cleared my mind and made way for ideas – some pretty good ones too."

"That's exactly how it works. Remember in high school how good you always felt after practice?"

Johnny felt himself redden slightly. "Did I mention that to you?"

"You didn't have to," Coach said. "Everybody feels that way."

Johnny chuckled. "Oh," he said. "Right."

"So that's energy, physical and mental. We'll talk more about that in detail, but for now let's move on to our second pillar, connections. We must create high quality connections in our personal and professional lives."

"Absolutely," said Johnny.

"You met your assistant, Susan, on the first day. Tom probably told you she is the oil that makes the engine of this team run so well. You recall meeting her?"

"Sure. We spoke briefly yesterday when I met with the rest of my team."

"Great," said Coach. "You remember her mentioning her ten-year-old, Curt, who has Down syndrome?"

"Yes, I remember."

"Susan has brought Curt with her, and I'd like you to meet him." He picked up the phone. "Susan, are you there?"

"Would you like to bring Curt into my office to meet Johnny? Great, thank you." Coach hung up the phone and smiled. "They'll be right down."

"Okay."

"Are you familiar with the Special Olympics?"

Johnny folded his hands in his lap. "I've heard of them. I know what they do, but I wouldn't really say I'm familiar with them."

"This company does a lot to support Special Olympics. We'll talk about it more after you meet Curt."

As if on cue, Johnny heard a knock at the door, and Coach called, "Come in." Susan entered, leading Curt, a tall boy with light blonde hair, by the hand.

"Hi Coach," said Curt.

"Hey Tiger," Coach said. "Curt, I'd like you to meet someone special. This is Johnny. He's going to be working with your mom."

Johnny stuck out his hand to shake Curt's small hand, but to his surprise and consternation, the boy threw his arms around him and hugged him tightly. He stood there for a moment and then patted the boy awkwardly on the back. It had been a long time since a child other than his own had given him a hug.

Curt let go and stood back. When he looked up at Johnny he said, "My mom said you were new to the company. Welcome to the team."

"Thank you," Johnny said. For a moment he wondered if this happened often. It seemed pretty unusual to have a child welcoming him to the team.

"I'm a golfer," Curt said, "and I run track too."

"Oh, that's great," Johnny said. He wasn't sure what else to say. While he and Curt were speaking, Coach and Susan exchanged a few words about some upcoming projects. When they had gone, Coach took Johnny aside again.

"One of the things I want to talk to you about today is the importance of connections. That is a quality connection right there."

Johnny smiled, feeling as though Coach was humoring him or perhaps just being generous. "Okay," he said.

"The thing is a person like Curt can change your life. Before we met him, all we knew was that he was one of Susan's children. But since meeting him, he's gone on to become someone who actually has been a great influence for NCI Systems."

Johnny knew how skeptical he must look as he asked, "Really?"

Coach stood with his hands behind his back looking out the window. "We like to be able to give back to the community in some way," he said, "and Special Olympics has become one of the organizations we are most involved with. They have their state summer games coming up, and we'll be participating for the third year in a row. Last year we raised almost thirty thousand dollars for them as a result of our fundraising efforts."

"Wow! I had no idea."

Coach smiled. "You know if you help others, you get back more than you ever give. That's the great thing about it."

"That's amazing."

"Yes," Coach said, "and it all starts with connections. So let's talk about your connections both professional and personal." He returned to the whiteboard and wrote:

"For our purposes professional connections don't just refer to your contacts list," said Coach. "High-quality connections is the term we use for short-term, dynamic, positive interactions at work.

"Think about the positivity of high-quality connections in terms of how you feel for people, what they do, and the benefits of the outcomes. Let me give you an example: Imagine how you feel when someone expresses concern for you after a long workday. They ask how you're doing, if you're okay, etc. That's a high-quality connection."

"Okay, got it," said Johnny.

"The foundation for a high-quality connection is based on three areas: cognitive, emotional, and behavioral mechanisms which explain how to determine the level of connection. Work connections are about the dynamic energy between two people when there's interaction involving mutual awareness.

"First of all, human beings are intrinsically social. We have a need to belong. Secondly, while we interact with each other, these connections are dynamic. They change as individuals themselves change how they feel, think, and behave. Third, we know that organizations perform work through social processes, and connections are key elements for the understanding of how work is accomplished.

Finally, we know that connections will vary in quality. Differences in quality reflect variance in how healthy and well-functioning the relationship is at a particular point in time. Are you following me?"

"Yes," said Johnny.

"One differentiation is the positivity of the people involved and the emotional experiences of each individual in the connection. Positive experiences impact the vitality of feelings in that connection," Coach said.

"Sure. I understand."

"People who have high-quality connections feel positive stimuli and a heightened sense of positive energy. Being positive denotes a sense of feeling known and loved or respected and cared for in the connection. That allows both people to feel movement in the connection and exposes vulnerability and responsiveness when full participation is experienced.

"Connectivity describes a connection level of openness to new ideas and influences. High-quality connections are important as a means for which people develop and grow. They are also associated with greater levels of psychological safety and trust. Higher levels of interpersonal trust enhance cooperation and trustworthiness. You understand that?"

"Absolutely."

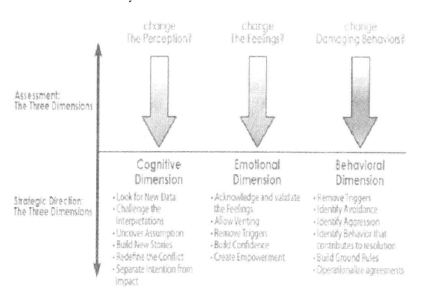

Coach continued, "Cognitive emotions highlight how conscious and unconscious thought processes predispose people to building high-quality connections. Emotional actions point out how feelings open people up to connection and are shared between people in ways that build high-quality connections. Behavioral actions determine how the two parties interact and share ideas and concerns. Like we see on this chart:

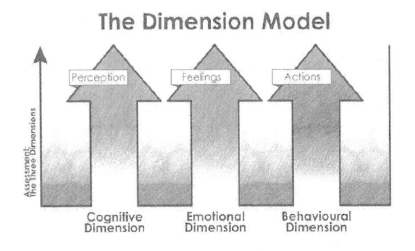

"Positive emotions broaden our thinking and help build durable, social resources," said Coach. "Gratitude or thankfulness happens when an individual perceives that someone intentionally provides something valuable to him or her. Feeling grateful towards others enhances attention to the positive qualities of both parties. When positive emotions are shared, the person receiving them unconsciously mirrors those of the other person."

"Okay," said Johnny. "This is important for me in my leadership role here, right?"

"Exactly," Coach said. "And I've got a little homework assignment for you tonight. In your playbook, look at this page. He flipped to the page indicated. "Come up with five personal and five professional relationships that you need to improve."

"Sure," said Johnny. "And that's to be completed for tomorrow?"

"The day after tomorrow. Meanwhile, take a look at this list of ways to positively connect employees to their leadership."

Coach showed Johnny a worksheet in his playbook with the following listed:

> **Ways to Positively Connect Employees to Leadership:**
> - Explain the overall organizational purpose and how each employee's job relates to it.
> - Include employees in the hiring process.
> - Be transparent & share things with employees.
> - Build an atmosphere in which employees have open communication.
> - Focus on developing employees.
> - Push employees in a positive direction in relation to job skills vs. knowledge.
> - Understand each employee's communication style.
> - Focus on internal customer service as much as external customer service.
> - Teach people to develop & take risks.
> - Disseminate information to all employees.
> - Motivate & create a sense of teamwork through team building.

Johnny read through the list quickly. "This is great," he said. "I've gotten plenty of suggestions about things such as these over the years, but this really crystallizes a lot for me."

"We really do emphasize team building here. That whole thing I mentioned just now about Susan and Curt and our participation in the state summer games?"

Johnny looked up from the list. "Yes, Coach?"

"We'll be starting that tomorrow."

14

SUMMER GAMES

The following morning, Johnny found himself driving to the university to participate in the Special Olympics State Summer Games. It wasn't even officially summer on the calendar, so he'd been surprised when Coach told him they were doing this today. He wondered what the event was going to be like.

Johnny's surprise grew even more when he arrived at a campus filled with cars and people. Competitors and their families, coaches, volunteers and spectators flooded the fields and parking lots.

Coach Davis, Charlie, Tom, Susan, Curt, and many other team members met him in the parking lot. Before long Johnny found himself in a one-to-one conversation with Coach.

"This is unbelievable. I never imagined an event such as this would be so big," Johnny admitted. "Talk about a great turnout."

Coach nodded. "It's really something. You know, the first year we did this, we were probably all just as surprised as you. Well, except for Susan and Curt."

"Why do we do it? I mean is it just to help Susan and Curt? Seems like a lot of effort and even money."

Coach smiled. "That's actually a good question. Yesterday you and I spent the first part of the day talking about professional connections, and today I want to talk to you a bit about personal connections."

"Okay."

Coach patted Johnny on the back as they walked along a few paces behind the rest of the group. "Johnny, if we want strong, high-quality connections in our personal lives, our communication with those most meaningful to us needs to be our top priority. Remember: To have a High Achiever Mindset your connections are an important part to living the life you want."

"I understand. But these are all fellow professionals here, right? I mean our relationships are more professional than personal."

"That's true, but some of these professional relationships have extended beyond and become friendships. Think about it. How many people do you know whose whole personal network is made up of people they work with? Their personal lives and professional lives are one and the same."

Johnny nodded. "You're right."

"We're not saying that you should do that. Far from it. But we have to be honest here. We're all going to be spending a lot of time together, so it's a good thing if some of those professional relationships become high-quality personal relationships. Heck, I was friends with Charlie for years before I even worked for the company."

"Gotcha."

"This extends way beyond the workplace. Think of your family. You want those personal connections to be as good as they can. Any other friendships you have can always be improved by emphasizing these high-quality connections: trust, gratitude, reciprocity. You can think of your own examples."

"Sure."

Coach shielded his face with one hand and squinted towards the field where the athletes would be competing. "You know, Johnny, one of the things that's happening right now is that connection and communication are being undermined by advances in technology. There's so much instant messaging, texting, and so forth that young people are rapidly losing their comfort level with good old-fashioned face-to-face communication. You're younger than me, but I know you're old enough to have some feelings about this too."

"Oh yeah," said Johnny. "I don't want my kids using their phones at the table. That's for sure."

"Well, that's excellent, and that's exactly what I recommend for families and friends. You're a step ahead. I have a simple three-step plan to help people connect daily with those closest to them:

SIMPLE THREE-STEP PLAN TO CONNECT:
1. Disconnect from technology and use face-to-face conversation.
2. Keep your breakfast and dinner tables free from electronic gadgets.
3. Don't multi-task when you're communicating with someone.

"We may feel that the art of true connection is being lost," said Coach, "but if you take the time to share your undivided attention with those closest to you, you'll never regret it."

By now the group had arrived at their destination. Curt was going to be competing in the 50-meter dash and the 100-meter dash, and Johnny was surprised to see that he was one of the younger contestants, who ranged from nine to over sixty. Coach continued as the group came to a stop.

"I'll tell you an interesting story about myself. Did you know I suffered a head injury when I was in grammar school?"

"No, I didn't. What happened?"

"I got hit with a baseball, and it caused what could have turned into an aneurysm. Long story short, I had to have a procedure, and the result was that I had to go to great lengths to protect my head after the surgery. That meant riding what we used to call the 'short bus' and wearing a batting helmet to school for a couple months.

"There was a young fellow on that bus who had Down syndrome and who tried to talk to me. He was very large, and I was much younger than him, so I was very small in comparison. I couldn't understand him, and he scared me."

"I see," said Johnny.

"The reason I'm telling you this is because as a young kid, concerned only with myself and my own fears and insecurities, I became afraid of people with developmental disabilities. What I didn't know yet and what I didn't learn until I was an adult is that I was lacking empathy to some degree."

"How do you figure?"

"Empathy is just the ability to identify and understand another person's situation, feelings, and motives. It's our capacity to recognize the concerns of others. You can see how I didn't have that for the young Down syndrome fellow."

"Ah, okay. Got it."

"Empathy keeps relationships running smoothly as it allows us to create bonds of trust, gives insights into what others may be feeling or thinking, helps understand how or why others are reacting to situations, sharpens our insights, and informs our decisions.

"Of course, I've got plenty of lists about all these topics, and here's another card I didn't get into your hands yesterday. This is in your playbook also."

"The more we use empathy, the stronger it becomes. Try some of these

TEN WAYS FOR BUILDING EMPATHY:

#1 Listen
#2 Don't interrupt
#3 Tune in to nonverbal communication
#4 Use person's name
#5 Be fully present
#6 Smile
#7 Encourage
#8 Give genuine recognition and praise
#9 Take personal interest
#10 Don't multi-task when communicating

suggestions and watch the reactions of others. I believe you'll see positive results in both your personal and professional relationships."

Johnny spent the day helping at the event, but more than that he made some new friends. At the end of the day, he drove home wondering what tomorrow would bring.

15

THE STRUGGLE

When Johnny arrived home, everyone was happy to see him, and he sank into his armchair exhausted from spending so much of his day in the sun.

"How was it?" Amy asked crouching down beside his chair with a hand on his arm.

"It was amazing," he said. "I never imagined so many people would be there for the games. Thousands upon thousands."

Amy arched an eyebrow. "Really? Sure you're not exaggerating just a tiny bit?"

He looked up. "No, I'm serious. It was packed. I got a lot out of it. Nicest bunch of people you'd ever want to meet."

"Glad you liked it," she said and stood back up. "Dinner will be ready in about thirty minutes."

"Thank you, honey."

During dinner Johnny told the children about the day's event.

"Kids, today I did something interesting: I volunteered with the Special Olympics."

"What's that?" Billy asked.

"I know," said Jack. "It's where they have a sports competition for special needs people."

"That's right," Johnny said. "And it was a great way to give back to the community. That's something I want us to be thinking about over the next few months. As a family what are we willing to support?"

The question led to a conversation about various charitable organizations. Johnny was proud to see how knowledgeable his children were about everything from the Red Cross to the United Way, and he felt more connected to them.

After dinner, though, he wasn't able to kick back and think about the next day. He had homework just like the kids.

He looked at the page: *Five Personal and Five Professional Relationships I Need to Improve On.*

Earlier in the day he'd felt inspired, but now his mind was as blank as the page before him.

Would it be cheating to list Amy and the kids as the first four personal relationships? He decided it was fine.

5 Personal:
1. AMY
2. JACK
3. BILLY
4. MARIE

5 Professional:
1.
2.
3.
4.

He tapped the pen idly against the paper. Who should be number five? His grandparents and parents had all passed. He thought of his sister, Sally, in Oregon. They hadn't spoken in months.

Then he looked at the second blank column. What would be the five professional relationships? He was brand new to the company. He figured he'd better be in good with Coach and Charlie, of course, but he was hard pressed to prioritize anyone else.

He thought of his assistant in the sales department. What was her name again? To his dismay he couldn't think of it. He pulled his phone from his pocket and began scrolling through the names.

He had to get all the way down to the letter *S* before he saw it and remembered Susan, Assistant to the Sales Team.

5 Professional:

1. COACH
2. CHARLIE
3. SUSAN
4.

He still had to come up with two more. As he tapped his finger idly against the phone, he glanced down at his full belly and remembered he had to go to the gym the next morning to meet his "accountability partner" Eric.

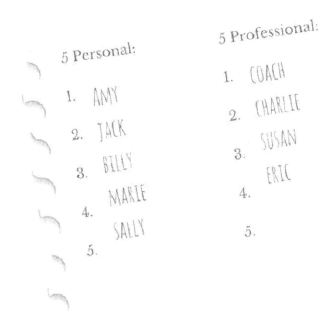

He sat back in the armchair with no idea for a final name. Tomorrow promised to be another long day.

16

INFLUENCING OTHERS

Johnny awoke an hour earlier than normal so he could meet Eric at the gym. He tried to shake the cobwebs out of his brain as he crawled into the car.

"This is insane," he thought. "It's still the middle of the night."

But he felt a little better after working out with Eric, who was all enthusiasm and energy, talking a mile a minute about how much weight he'd lost, how much better he felt, and how much he enjoyed exercise now. He encouraged Johnny by noting that Johnny was already far ahead of him at the beginning of his own get-back-in-shape journey.

Johnny knew he would be sore the following day, but he felt energized as he headed into the office. It was the first day he would be spending significant time with his team before meeting with Coach, and he wasn't sure how that would go.

The struggle began when Johnny tried to address the team about some ideas he had for restructuring their scheduling. Everyone seemed friendly and receptive to the new leader until this point, but Johnny could clearly see resistance from two employees, George and Mario. They crossed their arms, scowled, and shifted in their chairs with visible discomfort.

It was so obvious that even the other team members glanced over at the two men, so that Johnny felt obliged to address the issue right away.

"Mario, George, do you have questions?"

Mario smiled grimly. "Well, yeah. I mean, how do you know that that's even going to work for us? You're still in your first week of training here, right?"

"Yes, that's true, Mario," Johnny said and forced his own smile. "But I am the new leader, so I'd like to implement some things that I think will be effective for everybody."

"Did you do this at your last job?" asked George unsmiling.

"Yes, yes, I did," Johnny said.

"How did that work out for you?"

The room went deathly quiet, and Johnny felt himself flush. "Well, George, since you ask, I'll gladly tell you. That particular policy went perfectly fine, and it streamlined productivity. As you know, I did eventually leave that position but for other reasons. We'll table that discussion and return to it at another time."

On his way down the hall to meet Coach, Johnny found himself wondering about the resistance he had received and was surprised to think that maybe the problem wasn't with those employees or the way the company ran. Maybe it was more about him than the company. Maybe a couple of them are like that for a reason, he thought.

Johnny went in, said good morning, and immediately began to tell Coach about his struggles, the personal and professional relationships assignment, his energy in the morning, and the team just before their meeting.

"Interesting," said Coach. "Today we're going to talk about influence, so that will be appropriate."

"How do you mean?"

"Influence is the third pillar in The High Achiever Mindset," reminded Coach. "Our influence is either positive or negative. Ask yourself: What's the influence you want to show to those who are most important to you?

"We're going to talk about professional influences, but first let's talk about personal influence. We can all look back and find that one person who made an impact on our life. Take a moment, close your eyes, and think about that person. Mentally capture the person and visualize how they made a difference and influenced you. That influence has driven you to become who you are today.

"Who made the biggest impact on you?"

"You know, it's funny, but I think it was my grandmother on my mother's side."

"And why's that? What's funny?"

"I mean it's peculiar," Johnny said. "Of course, she spoiled me a bit, but it wasn't just that. I loved my parents, and they were great people, but they always had high expectations for me. My grandmother gave me unconditional love and never asked a thing from me."

"You have really hit on something, Johnny. Our life is not made of what we get but instead of what we give. I want you to take some time to inventory the influence you're giving to those most important relationships you've written in your playbook. To become a giver in these relationships, ask yourself these questions:

- Am I giving quality time to each of these relationships?
- Am I present when I am with these relationships?
- Do I give or take more from these relationships?
- What action do I need to take today to let these relationships know how important they are to me?
- When was the last time I genuinely thanked these relationships for who they are and what they mean to me?

"Write some short answers first, and you can expand on them over the next few days as you reflect and contemplate what you wrote. My last challenge is for you to become the influence you want to be in each of these relationships. As you share of yourself, you'll see your influence come back multiplied."

"What about professional relationships, Coach? I wasn't even sure who to write about other than you and Charlie. I added Susan and Eric after struggling with it for a while."

"Why don't you put Team on there for now? Then later go ahead and add all their names individually. I'd start with Mario and George if I were you."

Johnny grinned.

"People want to follow leaders who have a vision of where their company is going and how they uniquely contribute to its overall success," said Coach. "Lack of engagement is one of the biggest problems facing organizations today. If employees are fully engaged, they share in the dreams and goals of the organization. This allows them to take ownership in executing the vision of the company. Leaders often think sharing their vision once a year at a company meeting is enough, but to create true influence in your organization, you must share your vision daily.

"As organizations become increasingly global, the ability to influence others has become a must for leaders. When working across functions and geographies, leaders are often expected to produce results through people over whom they have no direct authority. Influence is turning your agenda into their agenda by gaining the commitment of others rather than forcing compliance."

"I see," said Johnny. "I'm afraid in the past at times I've been a little more on the forcing compliance side of the equation."

"That won't work here, Johnny. Influential leaders must become more agile in their interpersonal relationships. They want to employ the full range of influencing others' behaviors enabling them to project a new, more powerful image. They need to learn how to measure key colleagues, potential partners, fence-sitters, and adversaries and how to develop strategies for positioning their ideas and plans for acceptance by each group.

"Influence is more about self-awareness and the degree to which leaders are viewed as a powerful, influential leading force in their organization. This is accomplished by learning communication techniques for modifying or changing their image and becoming a stronger force without a commanding tone. Influence is also about understanding and navigating organizational politics or forces. Developing important degrees of cooperation from key colleagues is essential. Leaders need to develop an influence plan that enables them to achieve results from across the organization."

Coach referred Johnny to his playbook.

A list of ways to influence your team:
- Empower workers to complete tasks & hold them accountable.
- Develop systems for complete accountability.
- Build and work continually with maintaining trust.
- Make decisions based on the good of the organization, not just a select few.
- Learn how to effectively delegate to your team.
- Remove the barriers for your team's success.
- Identify & reward positive behaviors.
- Include your team with scheduling.
- Conduct honest, open performance evaluations every ninety days.
- Ensure that all leaders are conducting accountability with their teams.

"The influence in your team grows when you increase engagement with them," Coach reminded Johnny. "When you win over the hearts and minds of your team members, you will see them lead in ways that will lead our company to extraordinary efforts, which in turn will lead to positive financial results. To influence your employees be a visionary leader for your team and share the good and bad. When you are willing to be vulnerable and show everything, your team will rally to help create success in our organization. Vision can't stand alone; it must be supported with accountability from everyone on the team.

"Start with Mario and George, and go from there."

"I will, Coach."

"Finally, here is another card:

5 PRINCIPLES OF INFLUENCE:

#1 Enlarge people by learning.

#2 Navigate people from experience.

#3 Connect with people by understanding the art and science of leadership.

#4 Empower and develop people.

#5 Duplicate other leaders.

The Five Principles of Influence that will make a Difference in your Professional Relationships."

"Sounds like a plan, Coach. Thank you for all your help. What's next?"

"On Monday we will bring it all home with Integration."

17

INTEGRATION BEGINS

The following Monday Johnny walked into the conference room to find Coach.

"The final pillar in The High Achiever Mindset is integration," Coach began. "The key to successfully implementing integration is to first look at yourself. Integrating new habits and disciplines can be difficult. You must first decide to change and then set up a system to implement."

"Okay," Johnny said.

"People know how to start stuff but not how to finish it," Coach went on. "Let me ask you a question. What's your morning routine?"

Johnny chuckled, slightly embarrassed. "Well, we get the kids up and ready for school. It's a bit of a zoo, to be honest."

Coach grinned. "Do you get up before everyone else in your household?"

"No," he admitted.

"I'm going to suggest you get up before them all from now on," said Coach. "Even if that means you have to go to bed a little earlier. Make sense?"

"Sure."

"Here's my routine, which I call my Morning Magic Routine," said Coach, pulling a card from his pocket. "I've done this consistently for many years. See if you recognize yourself in any of these activities:

> **MORNING MAGIC ROUTINE:**
>
> - Rise by 5 A.M. on weekdays
> - 30 minutes spiritual time (reading, reflecting, & journaling)
> - Read 30 mins. (business development books)
> - Review Personal & Company Vision Statement
> - Review Personal & Company Mission Statement
> - Review Personal & Company Culture Statement
> - Practice Positive Affirmations
> - Journal for 15 minutes
> - Exercise 30-45 minutes daily

Johnny couldn't hide his surprise, nor could he help asking, "You journal, Coach?"

Coach laughed. "Remember when Charlie said I told him to journal about something every day for a week?"

"Yes, I do."

"Just as when I was coaching you guys on the football field, I'm never going to ask you to do something I wouldn't do myself."

"So I have to adopt these as part of my morning routine?"

"I want you to create better habits, Johnny. I'm not saying you have to clone this list, but you need to do more than you're doing now, and it all starts with your Morning Magic Routine. Then it builds from there."

"Okay."

"Integration is an extremely analytical, process-result oriented way of making decisions," said Coach. "Integration is about creating a culture which builds a direct, open, honest communication channel for all employees. It's about developing processes and systems that set the climate for performance of the organization in terms of expectations of individuals and departments.

"It would be foolish to establish a one-size-fits-all system for a company. It just doesn't work in today's workplace. The workplace today wants total accountability and strives to keep employees informed in all areas of the business. Organizations need to be transparent in their actions and beliefs."

Coach referred Johnny to the playbook again. "Take a look at this."

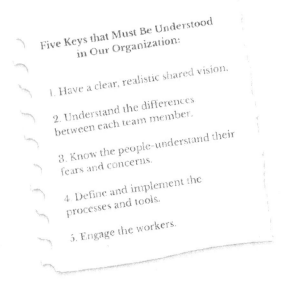

"Makes sense," said Johnny.

"Leadership needs to perform due diligence when communicating issues to employees," Coach continued. "That's especially important in a department such as yours where you're leading salespeople.

Employees will find out information about the organization before leadership is prepared to share if you do not have a communication plan. Do not ever lie to your team. When you can, share the information with them. It is imperative you do this. Holding back information only decreases the levels of integration within an organization and impacts employee loyalty and trust."

"I understand."

"Let's look at this list of integrations for your team."

Johnny looked at the next sheet Coach showed him in the playbook.

Integrations to Implement into Your Organization:
- Have clearly defined processes.
- All meetings should tie to goals/objectives of the organization.
- Monitor & communicate the budget.
- Communicate & track Key Performance Indicators (KPIs).
- Address issues in a timely manner.
- Update processes & accountability as needed.
- Support ongoing training, both personally & professionally, of your team.
- Empower your team.
- Have clear accountability.
- Follow through with promises.

"As you implement these integrations into the sales team, you'll see engagement improve. The goal is to increase the engagement of every person on the team, not just George and Mario. The team will then drive your culture, which in turn will drive the results of the organization. You follow me?"

"I follow you, Coach. And again, thank you."

18

PUTTING IT ALL TOGETHER

As the days turned to weeks, Johnny's new position with NCI Systems began to positively affect every area of his life. He continued to rise earlier than the rest of his family, started to enjoy the morning workouts with Eric, and became the leader he'd always wanted to be.

He knew he was on the right track at home when Amy said, "Honey, you need to get some new pants. Those are practically falling off you."

It was true. Johnny had lost almost ten pounds and was looking and feeling slimmer and more fit than he had in years. He patted his belly, which still had a little way to go. "Not bad, eh?" he said.

Amy smiled, drew closer, and put her arms around him from behind. "You're not only looking better, you're acting better. I don't know if it's the job, or if it's just being home and able to join us for church every Sunday. Maybe it's a combination of all of the above."

"Maybe so," he said. He turned around and gave her a hug and kiss. "I'm going to go in early again tomorrow. Big sales meeting."

"Go get 'em, tiger," she said, and they both chuckled.

The following morning Johnny arrived at the office about thirty minutes earlier than usual. He headed in to see if Coach had arrived because he wanted to chat with him for a few minutes before addressing the team. It would be an important meeting, and he needed to make sure he was doing things right.

Coach was already there. In fact, Johnny realized he'd never gotten to the office earlier than him. After they exchanged greetings, Johnny asked, "Coach, what time do you get here in the morning? It seems like you're never here later than me."

"I usually get in about six-thirty."

"Wow," Johnny said. "The office doesn't even open until eight-thirty. I thought I was early coming in at eight."

"Well, Johnny, it goes back to what I told you a few weeks ago. Go to bed a little earlier if you have to, and have that healthy Morning Magic Routine."

"Have you already done all those things in your routine before you even arrive here?"

"Not quite. Today I got a late start, so I still have to review our company statements. Care to join me for that?"

"Sure," Johnny said.

"Our Vision Statement says Success is dependent on taking care of our team members and guests. Our Mission is to create moments of magic for our internal and external guests in every interaction. And our Culture Statement is Guiding your ascension in business and life."

Johnny shook his head in amazement. "You've got those all down cold? You just memorized them?"

"I've read them over so many times, I don't even need to look at them. I memorized them without actually planning to do that."

"And your morning exercise?"

"Still doing about forty-five minutes. How about you? I seem to notice a few pounds off the old gut," he said.

Johnny laughed. "Doing well, doing well. Eric was the perfect accountability partner for me."

"Glad it's working out. What can I do to help you this morning?"

"Well, Coach, you know I have this big sales meeting today."

"Yes."

"I just want to make sure I'm motivating everyone. I think Mario and George have both fallen in line nicely, but

I want to make sure I'm on track with everything I'm doing."

Coach nodded. "Johnny, I'm not going to tell you how to do your job. I think you've got a good handle on our mission, vision, and culture. As long as you're coming from a place of helping your team succeed and doing it in a way that shows you understand that positive culture wins, I think you'll be fine today."

"Thank you, Coach. I will."

"I think we may have helped you find your true purpose."

"Oh, Coach, that reminds me. I wanted to share with you my purpose statement that I developed from your encouragement."

"Great, Johnny, please share."

Johnny unfolded a small piece of paper and read the following:

"MY LIFE'S PURPOSE IS TO BE A SERVANT LEADER. BY SHOWING APPRECIATION AND LOVE IN MY RELATIONSHIPS, I WILL HELP OTHERS GIVE OF THEMSELVES FREELY, LOVE OPENLY, AND MAKE A DIFFERENCE IN THE WORLD."

"Congratulations, Johnny. I can tell that your purpose comes from your heart. I told you the goal was to become the person God intended you to be.

"Have you seen some changes at home?"

"Yes, I have; in fact, Amy and I were just talking about that."

"I'm seeing them here too. You're a different man than the one I coached in high school, or even the one who accepted the position at NCI Systems. You're a better man." He checked his watch. "Now get in there and give your team all the help you can. You'll do just fine. You've been getting great results from them and from everyone else you've been around. I'm proud of you, Johnny."

To his surprise Johnny found himself moved almost to tears. He caught his breath. "Thank you, Coach," he said shaking his hand. "I really appreciate it."

"Johnny, thank you."

19

THE FUTURE

Twenty years came and went, and Johnny continued to work at NCI Systems. Twenty years of growth, happiness, and career fulfillment such as he had never known.

He and Amy were older now. They had their health, and the kids were all healthy too. It was hard to believe that Jack was twenty-eight, Bill was twenty-six, and Daddy's little girl, Marie, was a grown woman of twenty-four. Soon they were going to be grandparents as Jack's wife was expecting a boy in November.

Johnny sat in his office on a Friday afternoon. Most everyone had already gone home, but he was staying late to meet with a new employee.

How well I remember that feeling thought Johnny as he sat in the big leather office chair. Driving to a new job, stopping off at a fast food chain restaurant to grab a coffee, and rushing to the new job had been awful.

Johnny's assistant, Susan, had retired, and now he had a younger assistant, Jeanne. She was petite with curly black hair and very outgoing. He'd let her know he was expecting to speak with the new hire but sent her home at her normal hour. Typical for an NCI employee, she'd tried to insist on staying late.

"No, Jeanne, it's not a problem," Johnny told her. "I'm just having the front desk leave word to direct him to my office, and he can knock on the door. It's easy enough to find."

He reflected on his years at NCI Systems as he sat waiting in the big leather chair. How good it had all been! The principles of Energy, Connections, Influence, Integration, and The High Achiever Mindset seemed as timeless to him today as they had twenty years ago.

Now he had yet another opportunity to help a new person achieve his true life's purpose. It was beyond rewarding; it had become his vocation.

The knock at the door finally came. "Come on in," Johnny called out as he was looking out the window in contemplation. He heard the door open with a cautious creak. "Have a seat, David," said Johnny. David was in his early thirties with brown hair and a distinctive mustache.

The man came around Johnny's desk in a slow, tentative walk. Johnny looked up and smiled into the eyes of a man who looked a lot like Johnny himself had looked twenty years earlier: nervous, tired, a bit stressed out. He looked like someone who could use a friend, and he surely needed an accountability partner as he was a good forty or fifty pounds overweight.

Anxiously twirling his wedding ring around his finger, he stood in front of Johnny. Like Johnny, twenty years ago, David most likely had a wife at home who was just as unhappy as Amy had been back then.

"They told me I was to come see you, sir?" David said sitting carefully on the chair across from Johnny.

Johnny reached out a friendly hand to shake David's cold, sweaty palm. "Yes," he said. "Pleased to meet you, David. I'm Coach Johnny. I'm here to help."

20

PUTTING THE HIGH ACHIEVER MINDSET TO WORK

As you reflect about the struggles and triumphs Johnny experienced throughout the story, Ascend Business Strategies hopes you have already begun to implement The High Achiever Mindset principles into your life and business.

At this stage there are two possible types of readers:

1. Those who have read the text and are anxious to start implementing some of the principles. Congratulations. You're on the way to achieving your true life's purpose. You can get helpful downloads, tools, and resources free of charge at: **www.PositiveCultureWins.Biz.** I have also created a complimentary 7-Day CHARGE Program to assist you in this journey. You will find out more information about this program on the next few pages.

2. Those who have read through the book and do not plan on taking any action. We know from experience that some people will do this, and that's okay. We strongly encourage you to put these strategies to work. If you have questions or do not know where to start, feel free to contact me at **gwilbers@goascend.biz**

Johnny didn't become the new coach overnight, and you won't get results right away either. However, with a positive mindset and true dedication to making your life better, you can grow as he did. We wish you the very best on your journey to ascension in your business and life.

CONTACT GARY

Gary Wilbers is a High Performance Coach, Speaker, and Trainer. He works with organizations to transform the challenges leaders and teams face in regards to change and growth. Gary has been a successful entrepreneur and owner of multiple businesses in Missouri since 1990. He studied entrepreneurs such as Sam Walton, Brendon Burchard, Brian Tracy, and Charles Red Scott. He learned their principles and then built his own roadmap for success which he shares as he helps leaders develop into High Achievers.

For more information on Coaching, Training, and Keynote Speaking, contact Gary:

Phone: (573) 644-6655 **Email:** GWilbers@GoAscend.biz
Online: www.goascend.biz

Ascend Business Strategies

1731 Elm Court Jefferson City, MO 65101

To purchase bulk copies of this book at a discounted rate, please contact Gary Wilbers:

gwilbers@goascend.biz or (573) 644-6655

7 DAYS TO CHARGE
(Create Habits Around Real Goals Everyday)

Thank you for reading Positive Culture Wins. To show my appreciation I am giving you my **FREE** seven-day video series program valued at $97. This program will help you with the first steps of implementing CHARGE into your daily life. You will receive one email daily for seven days. Each will contain a short video and a resource to help you begin to create a life of CHARGE.

To begin, go to **www.PositiveCultureWins.Biz**

Your seven-day journey consists of

Day 1: Foundation: The obstacles of getting CHARGE into your everyday life.

Day 2: Mindset: Are you in the Climber or Stuck Mindset?

Day 3: Energy: The Energy you need each day comes from within you.

Day 4: Connections: What relationships need your attention?

Day 5: Influence: Your Influence is shown each day by your actions.

Day 6: Integration: Which habit or disciplines do you need to start today?

Day 7: Great Results/Purpose of Life: When you start living a life of CHARGE, you will realize you are living for purpose.

ABOUT THE AUTHOR

Gary Wilbers has been an entrepreneur and owner of multiple businesses in Missouri since 1990. He created an acronym that has shaped his life's foundation: CHARGE: Create Habits Around Real Goals Everyday. He studied entrepreneurs such as Sam Walton and Charles Red Scott and learned their principles. Then he built his roadmap for personal success.

The first business Gary built, Mid-America Wireless, started as a small two-man company and culminated with ten regional storefronts and over one hundred and fifty employees. He developed a culture of learning and a sharing of knowledge within his companies. His goal and commitment were to always make a team member better equipped than when he/she started. Gary created a framework, The High Achiever Mindset, using his success as the foundation. He now shares his message as a keynote speaker, trainer and coach in order to help others reach their goals, dreams, and ambitions. Gary is a certified High Performance Coach from the High Performance Institute.

Gary is also involved in his community, giving his time and resources to several organizations. His passion is working with Special Olympics Missouri. He currently serves on the statewide board and served as the Capital Campaign Chair for the Training for Life Campus fund drive with the purpose of building a state-of-the-art facility for Missouri athletes. One of his greatest joys is playing unified golf with Keith Lueckenhoff, a SOMO athlete.

Gary and his wife Dana have three children: Chris, Adam and Elle and reside in Wardsville, MO.

CITATIONS

Chapter images provided by PresenterMedia.com-
http://presentermedia.com/

Book cover image designed by Iconicbestiary – freepik.com, "people standing together in shape of an arrow,"
Freepik.com, www.freepik.com/index.php?goto=74&idfoto=1311194

Book cover design by UMAKANT-
https://designers.designcrowd.com/designer/120318/uk

Made in the USA
San Bernardino, CA
18 March 2018